Press-Ganged:
Journalism's shaky start to the Digital Age

Mike Scialom

"No former period, in the history of our Country, has been marked by the agitation of questions of a more important character than those which are now claiming the attention of the public"
– From the manifesto accompanying the launch of the *Manchester Guardian*, May 5, 1821

"When enough people make false promises, words stop meaning anything, and there are no more answers, only better and
better lies, and lies won't help us in this fight"
– 'Jon Snow' (Kit Harington), Game of Thrones

For my family and friends

Chapter 1: History

Chapter 2: Boarding school

Chapter 3: Computer games

Chapter 4: Future Publishing

Chapter 5: Transition

Chapter 6: Cambridge Evening News

Chapter 7: Subs desk

Chapter 8: Changing of the guard

Chapter 9: On the books

Chapter 10: Motoring

Chapter 11: Road test

Chapter 12: New century

Chapter 13: Fleet Street

Chapter 14: Disaster

Chapter 15: Post 9/11

Chapter 16: Phoney war

Chapter 17: Walkout

Chapter 18: 'Sword of Damocles'

Chapter 19: Bizmag

Chapter 20: Business writer

Chapter 21: The "never-never" forever

Chapter 22: Churn

Chapter 23: Phenomenon

Chapter 24: Local World

Chapter 25: IT

Chapter 26: Trinity Mirror

Chapter 27: The Cambridge Independent

Chapter 28: The Afghans on the bus

Chapter 29: EU referendum

Chapter 30: Picked off

Chapter 31: Cambridge Open Media

Chapter 32: Wellbeing disequilibriums

Chapter 33: Freelancing

Postscript: Fightback

Preface

In the digital age if you're not a disruptor you're going to be disrupted and for much of this century the newspaper industry has fallen on the wrong side of the divide.

The last 20 years have been the most fraught for print in generations. Convulsive changes have occurred so fast there hasn't been time for the underlying narrative to be apprehended, but the danger is now all too apparent. The newsprint sector has struggled to successfully port its business model on to the internet at the same time as serious attempts have been made by bankers – aided and abetted by a majority of politicians – and the ultra-rich to delegitimise the press as an entity. The trade was wrong-footed by the internet and then out-gunned by Silicon Valley, and along the way was highjacked by powerful corporations who preferred to use the media to promote – or conceal – their own interests. Now – somehow – the trade has to pick itself up and battle on.

There has been progress, of course. Newspapers' role as a disseminator of verified information has been successfully recreated online in terms of readership, but digital advertising revenues for newspapers have nowhere near offset the downturn in print sales and print advertising revenues. The trade's policy to the dangers it faced was to cut overheads, which masked the loss of profitability and created unhelpful outcomes for both newsroom headcounts and the quality of the product. A decade's worth of budget cuts has negatively impacted the ability of the fourth estate to do its job of serving the public interest by holding power to account.

As the roll-out of digital architecture has progressed many newsroom roles have been elided, ever-higher story counts demanded and digital traffic targets continuously circulated. Workloads are such that it becomes too time-consuming to leave the newsroom during the working day, further weakening the connection with the paper's readership.

As this has happened, the ability to write "without fear nor favour" has been progressively undermined by proprietors of national newspapers requiring their publications to back an editorial line which served their own, rather than their readers', interests.

However, a breach of faith between publisher and journalist is one thing: a breach of faith between journalist and reader is quite another. "Reputation arrives on foot and leaves by horse," goes the saying. The weakening of this hard-fought for bond between writer and reader began in earnest during the run-up to the Iraq War in 2003, when journalists were confronted with the industrial use of a new political weapon: spin. Spin saw the UK government's media teams, led by Alastair Campbell, playing some pretty desperate cards but it didn't mean that journalists bought into the deceptions and diffusions that characterised the new spin doctors' output. That capitulation was more subtle, as newspaper ownership resulted in titles unquestioningly adopted the agenda of their political and corporate masters. When combined with the requirement that journalists pursue high levels of digital traffic to save their jobs, the untangling of truth from fiction has become time-consuming.

At the very time journalism most needed to be free and fair, it became ever more tangled up in financial, technological and cultural dynamics which prevented it from doing its job effectively. Could this process have been deliberately encouraged? Inflicting damage to the media's ability to investigate and report on events suits those who would skew the public's understanding and awareness of economic and cultural issues. By significantly altering the capacity and ability of journalists to do their jobs, stories which journalists of another era would have been able and willing to write went unrecorded or were under-researched. Through the blizzard of spin, propaganda, fakery and 'alternative facts', a new breed of press baron in the UK has been shaping titles to suit their personal agendas of low taxation and low state spending. The result, according to a YouGov poll in 2016, is that the British press is now the "most right-wing" and "biased" in Europe.

This bias encouraged delusions which have divided and weakened the country. The outcome has been a surrender of economic and cultural prestige unimaginable at the close of the 20th century. A not dissimilar process across the Atlantic has combined to fragment the West's ability to address the far more urgent issues of climate change and economic inequality. This process has – perhaps unwittingly – contributed to the increased power and financial muscle of Russia and China. That this has happened on our watch needs to be explained, not to try and reanimate past glories, but to inspire an imperilled public to consider the dangers as well as the opportunities of the new age we find ourselves in.

The first newspaper to go online in the UK was the *Daily Telegraph* in 1994, but the pages were only updated once a day and dwell time – the amount of time spent reading an individual item – was very low due to the expense of pay-by-minute internet access. The first Google search took place in 1998, at which point there were 147 million world-wide internet users. By 2005 there were a billion internet users and by 2017 3.9 billion – more than half the world's population.

The digital era picked up speed with astonishing ferocity but, even so, it wasn't until 2006 that the *Guardian* introduced a "web-first" policy which reflected the 24-hour news cycle that began in 1989 with the launch of Sky News (the BBC's 24-hour news channel started in 1997). Today many newspapers post content digitally first, even though the online revenue stream exposes the pretensions of the trade in a harsh new economic landscape. If, for instance, I want to buy some new furniture, am I really going to go to a newspaper site for ideas, or am I going to google 'furniture'? At what point does the trade conclude that the Holy Grail – of digital revenue overtaking print revenue – isn't working out too well, and start to develop a coherent billing model, perhaps one which extracts value from the stories themselves as its first priority?

At the *Cambridge News* (the *Cambridge Evening News* until 2007), where I was happily employed from 1996 to 2017, the changes were initially relatively glacial. The newspaper's website went live in 2002: for its first few years it was populated by a copy inputter, Becky Harris, who typed in the stories directly from the print edition before the email system developed enough to have the text submitted to her by email. Halcyon days! The first digital editor was Rachel Extance, the title's erstwhile news editor, who took on the new role in 2007. From that point on the newsroom's focus and skillsets were progressively redirected towards producing online content that was traffic-friendly. If this was a cookery school, the menu gradually was gradually devolved from something close approximating gourmet to fast food.

By the middle of the second decade of the new century, the trade's digital editors and analysts had been elevated to the status of high priests of the new technology, and journalists were relegated to the position of outliers in their own trade. But even if the new cadre hugely boosted the number of browsers, the long-promised revenue stream stubbornly refused to materialise. Not their fault perhaps, but by 2015 the window – of successfully pivoting into the digital nirvana that Facebook and Google enjoyed – had been and gone.

At the coal face, faith in the new technology was replaced by anxiety. As the industry scrambled to develop a fully functional financial model, publishers scrabbled around for ways to ensure continued interim profitability. Cuts of increasing savagery were implemented right across the board and, to sustain the idolatry for ever-increasing digital traffic figures, the daily story count went up, though there were fewer journalists and the amount of time that could be spent writing a story was reduced to just a handful of minutes.

No business model for newspapers can afford to exclude digital from its strategy, but it's not heresy to say that the sector has yet to develop a cross-industry revenue model that satisfies the reader, the journalist and the publisher. Though a new payment model is proposed here – indeed, it is a key purpose of publishing this pamphlet – the eventual outcome will require more than merely a financial solution. A public relations campaign will be needed to rebrand journalism in the context of the social function it performs. The industry's collective voice needs to be heard because, while newspapers are struggling to hold the powerful to account, society is disintegrating. Emotional, physical and mental health are nosediving; poverty and homelessness are rocketing; incomes – except those at the top – are going down and social mobility is in reverse.

Reading will always be a crucial component of the world we live in. News is part of the glue that binds us together, and society benefits from the information and insights that newspapers provide. Readers need to be properly informed about the time and skill it takes to write a news story, especially when research and/or interviews are involved. It is beyond irony that the fate of newspapers in the last 20 years has been so under-reported. For instance, I live and work in Cambridge. It's a successful city and we're lucky to have two local newspapers. There's lots to report: there are phenomenal advances in technology and medicine happening here all the time. Developments taking place in and around the city in the fields of artificial intelligence, the Internet of Things, genomics, pharmaceuticals and technology are all taking place at great speed and should be part of the national conversation because, without dialogue and understanding, decisions will be made and roads chosen without any public scrutiny or awareness.

It takes time to acquire information from sources and pull the strands together for a report. It's in everyone's interests that journalism succeeds. Good journalism – even basic good journalism – saves society a lot of money further down the road, and this effort spent sourcing stories, collating information, interviewing those involved and writing up notes takes as long as it ever did.

We probably haven't got all that much time but, even if it all goes belly-up next week, it's already been a fascinating journey and – for now – we've still got tomorrow to try and sort it out...

– Chapter 1 –

The story of writing began in around 3,500-3,000BC when the Sumerians in Mesopotamia developed cuneiform, a word derived from the Latin 'cuneus', which means 'wedge'. The system involved a writing implement – a stylus – being passed through soft clay to produce trenched impressions: these were initially pictographs, followed by the hieroglyphs of ancient Egypt and Crete in around 3,000BC. (Chinese script was developed in about 1,600BC, independently of the Middle Eastern scripts.) Their primary function was to keep tabs on the amounts and values of the grain being stored and sold as settlements developed.

Cuneiform was in use until 100BC when it was replaced by the first alphabetic script.

Until around 1440, when Johannes Gutenberg invented the printing press, reading remained largely the domain of the clergy, though the administrative orders were increasingly using manuscripts to record exchanges. Pre-Gutenberg, literacy levels have been estimated to be around one in five in towns – one in 20 in the countryside.

The first newspaper was published in Germany in 1605. Others followed in the Netherlands and France. The first English-language newspaper was printed in Amsterdam in 1620 – probably because the right to print was strictly controlled in England. Spain, Portugal and Sweden all had their own newspapers by the mid-17th century. America's first newspaper was published in Boston in 1690.

The first title published in England was the *Oxford Gazette*, which appeared in 1665. The first daily newspaper was the London-based *Daily Courant*, which began printing in 1702. By 1720 there were 12 newspapers being printed in London and 20 printed regionally. By the early 19th century this had risen to 52 London papers and 100 other titles around the country.

The Times started life as *The Daily Universal Register* in 1785 and changed its name in 1788. In 1814 the publishers acquired a press capable of making 1,100 impressions an hour, and this was soon adapted to print on both sides of the paper at once, making the title cheaper and more widely available. This accessibility went up a notch in 1830 when the first 'penny press' went on sale: newspapers had their first taste of the mass market.

Sales picked up rapidly when publishers realised they could hook in readers by printing instalments of novels. The first was Charles Dickens' 'The Pickwick Papers', which appeared in 1836 and proved a huge success. In the United States, 'Uncle Tom's Cabin' was published over a 40-week period by *The National Era*, an abolitionist periodical, in 1851. It too was a runaway success. Reading was catching on big-time, and what you read would become the talking points of your day. By 1890 in England the *Daily Telegraph* had a circulation of 300,000.

The original national halfpenny paper in Britain was the *Daily Mail*, followed by the *Daily Express* and the *Daily Mirror*, which became the first weekday paper to pass the one-million sales milestone in 1911. Globally, newspaper circulations continued to increase, reaching a peak in the UK during the

1950s when the *News of the World* sold eight million copies every Sunday.

By 2014, no UK newspaper had sales of more than two million a day, although at the time of writing the *Sun* and the *Daily Mail* still sell about 1.5 million copies a day – which isn't too bad for an industry supposedly in decline.

The story of newspapers in the last 20 years is the story I am hoping to tell, using the lens of my own experience at one of the nation's most successful regional titles, the *Cambridge News* (the *Cambridge Daily News* from 1888 to 1969, and the *Cambridge Evening News* from 1969 to 2007). But how I got caught up in the restructuring of journalism in the 21st century – or should that be the de-structuring of news in the 21st century – is part of the story too.

– Chapter 2 –

We were a *Daily Express* household as a child. It was the UK's most-read newspaper for many years, selling around four million copies every day. The arrival of the *Sunday Express* was a high point of the week – we didn't have a television until I was in my teens and there were only three radio stations, all run by the BBC. My lifelong love of newspapers accelerated in the 1970s, when I was a boarder at a public school in Hertfordshire, an hour's drive from the family home in north London.

There was little for a 13-year-old to do at boarding school of a weekend: some would read or study, the sportier types would be outside the boarding house playing football or cricket, and for everyone else it was a question of finding a way to fill the hours. Table tennis was one option, and I became an extremely good table tennis player. Other than that? We were allowed to watch TV for two hours on a Sunday, which generally meant a football game – *The Big Match* was on ITV on Sunday afternoons, and seats were at a premium. The older boys got first dibs, so the younger ones were left out on a limb. The only other diversion was the arrival of the Sunday papers on the common room table: the *Mail on Sunday, Sunday Express, Sunday Telegraph* and the *Sunday Times*.

The *Sunday Times* stood out: it was edited at the time by the magnificent Harold Evans who, between 1967 and 1981, navigated the paper through a bewildering set of issues with astonishing sure-footedness. Newspapers were changing: in

1966 *The Times* had stopped using the whole of its front page for classified advertising, which opened the floodgates to headlines, stories and pictures.

The *Sunday Times' Insight* team set a new bar for newspaper writing, taking investigative journalism to the height of its powers with visual and written coverage of all major world events including the thalidomide medical scandal, the Vietnam and Yom Kippur wars, and Watergate, which brought down the US president, Richard Nixon. All were covered forensically, both in terms of the facts and in terms of possible interpretations of the facts.

Under Evans' stewardship, photojournalism had an almost insurrectionist approach to reporting the news. The vibrancy and energy of photographs in the paper and the magazine was a stunning rebuff to an era still emerging from monochrome. Most TVs received only black and white images. I didn't even see TV in colour until 1970, when I watched the live quarter final of the World Cup between England and Brazil at a friend's house. It was a revelatory experience, but basically I grew up with the radio and newspapers as my only access to the outside world, and juniors weren't allowed radios at boarding school.

The *Sunday Times* empowered a generation, informed us that we were a part of a wider world, and even seemed to hint that our opinions – if we could formulate arguments and present them in ways which would be heard – mattered. It was a world I had little access to from the countryside of Hertfordshire. Though I knew one day I would have to find my way in that wider world, I had no idea how I would fit in or even what steps I could take towards it.

Journalism seemed impossibly glamorous to a bored teenager in a rural boarding school. It never occurred to me to consider it as a job: the understanding of going to boarding school was that one would go on to a successful career in lawyer or medicine. The traditional route into journalism – joining a local paper as a junior reporter and working up from there – completely passed me by. I never knew such a path even existed until my former school chum Adrian embarked on it a decade later. But then, in some ways I had a rather sheltered childhood.

– Chapter 3 –

The first escapades I had in the world of work brought mixed fortunes. Like most people in their teens in London in the 1970s, I just wanted to get on with it, with no clue about what the "it" might involve. As "it" turned out I took two gap years, working as a hospital porter for the first, and travelling overland – there and back – to India for the second, after which I set off to Manchester to do a psychology degree. Three years later I was back in London looking for a job, still with no specific agenda in mind, other than to do something creative if possible.

It was in Manchester, in 1979, that I first encountered a computer. Until then technology meant the abacus, the slide rule, and the calculator. However, in a laboratory in the statistics department sat a green-screen Commodore Pet, with a full keyboard, and a printer. The Pet had 4kb RAM and 16kb ROM – one millionth of the memory on a basic iPhone today – was mostly used to crunch numbers for the statistics component of the course, but one evening I was working late and asked the technician if the Pet could do anything other than crunch numbers. He replied that it could play chess. I was gobsmacked – chess? How could a machine do the thinking involved in a game of chess? I asked the technician to set up a game, which he did. It was astonishing to see the chess board on the screen with all the pieces rendered into a digital format, with one of the squares blinking at you, awaiting your next move – or rather, your next instruction.

Once I understood how to move the pieces around the screen I found out that not only could the Pet play chess, but it was very proficient, and I was beaten far more times than I won. I went home in a state of turmoil, even anguish: my father had taught me to play chess to a very high standard, and I felt like I was letting him down somehow, so I tried to work out how a calculating machine could be scaled up to achieve chess mastery. I was both outraged and incredulous: slowly, it became clear that the machine was working out every possible move methodically, and deciding on the best option – one that minimised damage to its own position and at the same time caused maximum damage to its opponent. To do this the computer had to calculate as many moves ahead as possible. How many? And how many moves ahead was a human brain capable of calculating? And how many was I capable of calculating!? I spent many evenings – including, it must be said, many in the pub – trying to figure out how a computer could be set up to think faster, more efficiently, and more accurately (for chess at least) than a human brain.

With none of these thoughts in mind, I became a salesman for a Prestel company based in the City of London. Prestel was the first digital news service, built for TV. It was an early form of news feed. A channel on your TV screen displayed static news stories, and my job was to sell the advertising that went alongside these stories. It was a commission-only job and there were weeks when I would earn £600, and weeks I took home £50. But in the City in the 1980s everything was changing and it felt that perhaps great things were possible.

Greatness eluded me, or perhaps I eluded it, but the notion that it was proximate was good enough – for a while, at least.

In the summer of 1982 I met Lee, who became my first business partner. Lee had worked for Island Records and managed bands. Then he'd had a bad car crash. He was still recuperating: the Prestel job was part of his journey back into the world of work. Having just turned 30, and with business experience at or near the top level already on his CV, he was exploring other options.

Lee was never short of ideas: he was planning to move to LA to launch a new publishing venture in time for the LA Games in 1984. After an initial visit Stateside he mentioned starting a company selling a new home computer, but it seemed an unlikely punt. I went along with the plan because I'd learned to value Lee's ability to spot opportunities.

The company was to be called Micro Dealer UK and would sell a computer designed by one of Clive Sinclair's team, which was based in Cambridge. Clive Sinclair had started the home computing revolution with a kit computer called the ZX81. It was for hobbyists, as was the ground-breaking Sinclair Spectrum which followed it in 1982. One of Sinclair's designers, Richard Altwasser, had become disaffected and left to design his own computer, the Jupiter Ace.

As it turned out the Ace was a dud. I got one to play around with at home: I had to learn a computer programming language, Forth, to get anything to happen because there was no software on sale. It was laborious and boring, and after many hours I could only get a block to move around the screen. This was years behind the chess-playing Commodore

Pet! But as I started looking around for what sort of software was out there for other formats, it became clear that computer games was already a very vital and fast-developing cottage industry.

Lee had a chum called Neil Johnson, and together we bought £13,000 worth of cassette-based computer games software. Lee and Neil put in £5,000 each, and I contributed £3,000, which was all I could manage, and most of that was borrowed. What happened next was phenomenal – we turned over £1 million in the first year of trading. From a standing start with a few boxes in Neil's Hounslow home-turned-office, we were suddenly selling computer games to retailers all over Europe, from large chains to small independents. It was absolute pandemonium: my first experience of being an entrepreneur began with vertical growth, a once-in-a-lifetime adrenalin trip which bonded us together like we were rock stars or astronauts.

Lee and Neil proved shrewd strategists, and after the first couple of hugely successful trading years they took the company on to an USM listing. The Unlisted Securities Market was a minor stock market for firms getting ready for a full listing which operated from 1980 to 1996 in the City of London. The USM listing was achieved by a reverse takeover of another, larger company, the Spectrum Group, which sold cameras from dozens of shops all over the UK. It was an audacious move, but Lee and Neil had fantastic complementary skills.

With stock market money in the bank, we had to find ways to spend it. Each of us was expected to come up with an idea. I'd seen a trade magazine in the video sector, *Video*

Trader, courtesy of my girlfriend at the time, Jo, who was its deputy editor. *Video Trader* had already experienced the sort of vertical trajectory the computer games market was experiencing and it seemed like a good idea to do something similar for the home computer market, so my plan was to start a trade paper for the computer games sector and call it *Computer Trade Weekly,* which I would edit. It was a brazen move for someone with no experience of journalism, but I was restless and didn't want to keep working alongside Neil and Lee forever, plus there was enough cash in the firm to bankroll a speculative venture. I figured they might welcome being shot of me, too, because the shares I owned were turning out to have value in terms of influence as well as money, and I was light years away from their level of business acumen.

We had a meeting at which the proposal was discussed. There was a silence when I finished, then Neil said: "It's very interesting that you should have come up with this suggestion, Mike." He pulled out a file with "Home Computer Trade Weekly" on it and put it down on the table, and the contents almost exactly matched *Computer Trade Weekly* in terms of editorial and advertising strategies.

We had a discussion, starting off with "great minds think alike!" banter and then moving on to my role. I insisted that I should be made launch editor, swatting away any nervousness from Lee and Neil by proposing that we hire a trained reporter as my deputy. This was followed by a decision on whether the title should include "Home" or not. I said no, because it limited our scope to cover other areas of computing as they came along. Microsoft, for instance, had a program called *Flight Simulator* out for the PC, which was a huge success, allowing those who wanted to learn how to fly a plane to make a start on their computer. This wasn't software for a "home" computer, and we should definitely be covering the wider market, was my argument. In the end the debate was settled by Neil, who accepted having a small "Home" sticker across a big masthead which read "Computer Trade Weekly". It was a face-saving exercise and we all knew it, and the "Home" sticker was dropped after a couple of months.

I was glad to get out of Micro Dealer. My role had become sales-based and I was desperately bored. I kept my shares for a while longer, though. They would come in useful later.

Computer Trade Weekly (*CTW*) became a runaway success from the first edition of its two-decade shelf life. The suggestion that we hire a trained journalist as my deputy who would help with the production and legal aspects of publishing resulted in the recruitment of a young reporter from *Smash Hits* (a hugely popular tabloid pop magazine in the 1980s) called Greg Ingham.

The first few months were a steep learning curve. I got a desk with a typewriter on it, and a telephone, and my own coffee mug. That was the technology in those days, and an ashtray for the smokers: smoking in offices in those days was something you were obliged to negotiate as best you could whether you were a smoker or non-smoker.

It was quite easy to chat to my chums in the games trade and make a story out of whatever they said. The sector was still in its Wild West days, and there were some amazing games appearing, but also lots of bankruptcies and firesales as firms overstretched or devoted themselves to formats which weren't selling. The Sinclair Spectrum, Commodore 64 and BBC micro were the hot sellers on the hardware front.

As it turned out Greg was hugely competent, and his writing style was snappy and lean, which everyone responded to well and, through sheer enthusiasm combined with an extensive personal knowledge of the market and its key figures, I was able to masquerade as a journalist with some success. But who was the pupil and who was the master? Rather late in the day, I realised I hadn't been made editor, I'd been made "launch editor". Big difference. The editor gets to have his feet under the table, the launch editor has a far briefer trajectory. He parachutes in, claims the runway, then leaves it to others to develop. My first harsh lesson in business contracts taught me the value of always reading what's in front of you, not what you want to be in front of you.

After 18 months it became apparent that Greg could be a hugely capable editor in his own right, and I started to feel awkward, so I cashed out my shares and left the business I'd co-founded.

A few years later Micro Dealer was sold to the media mogul Robert Maxwell, who owned the Mirror newspaper group, and he turned it over to the group's computer software firm, Mirrorsoft, who quietly let the business atrophy until it was disbanded in the early 1990s. Lee and Neil were well out of it by then: Lee was living in Australia with his wife, Bella, and Neil had disappeared. The last I heard he'd been told by his accountant that his finances were in such a mess he needed to disappear for a while. South America may have been his destination but, after that, the trail runs cold.

By this time – 1986 – Jo and I were married and we had two young girls, Emily and Florence, in tow. Jo wanted to move away from London and its relentless city rhythm so, both aged 28, we moved to Somerset, to a small town called Street, famous only for its shoe company, Clarks, and for having a little town with a global footprint called Glastonbury just along the road.

I'd been to Glastonbury before, in fact I'd had an amazing experience there five years previously. I'd heard from an old school buddy called Nick who had moved to Australia and was back in the UK on a rare visit. He didn't have much time in his diary but I could join him on a Vipassana course in Wiltshire if I fancied it?

Vipassana is a Buddhist-based programme where you go on a ten-day retreat which involves not talking for the whole ten days, getting up at 5am to start meditating, not reading anything nor listening to any music. It's the most extreme form of Buddhist practice. I said yes, did the Vipassana course – just – and as we were leaving Nick said he was going to Glastonbury to visit a spiritualist organisation called the White Brotherhood and would I like to go along too? I was up for it.

So we arrived in Glastonbury one evening, after dark, and booked into a guest house called Tor Down. At 4am I woke up, fully alert, and had an intuition – so strong it was almost a voice – which suggested a walk up the hill. I looked out of the window and could just make out the Tor looming over the house. It felt like being in *Lord of the Rings*.

I set off up the hill, arriving at the top half an hour before dawn, and sat down near the famous tower. And dawn was the most spectacular event, with the surrounding countryside becoming slowly visible, but immediately around the Tor the clouds didn't disperse, and you could hear the sheep underneath the mist baa-ing as the birds flew around above the fug. It was an astonishing scene and Glastonbury was properly on my radar after that. I welcomed the idea of moving there: it would be a new adventure.

Within days of moving to Street, I had a phone call from someone I'd never heard of but who had heard of me. Chris Anderson had just started a publishing company in the next town, Somerton, producing computer games magazines. Would I like to get involved? I was less than enthusiastic. I'd left the computer games industry and was starting to think that it was an inappropriate line of business for me to be in, but Chris said: "Look, you can work a couple of days a week if you like, it would be great to have you on board."

So off I went to Somerton, met Chris who I really liked, and it was agreed that I would become the news editor of his latest magazine, *PC Plus*, for two days a week. This, my second job in journalism, made me feel like I had my foot in the door, even if I didn't want to open it too wide. I reviewed computer games, interviewed people, talked the talk and wrote – partly in jest – an edgy column called Ziggurat about how the computer world would trigger a dystopia in permanent meltdown. Sort of *Black Mirror* in print.

It was a lot of fun putting *PC Plus* together and Chris, who went on to be the curator of the TED Talks format, had a great sense of visual flair which was incredible to observe. He made some crazy calls, like rejigging the cover an hour before deadline, but when you saw the cover on the newsstand it would be a light year ahead of everything else in terms of energy and appeal.

Future Publishing was growing super-fast and soon outgrew Somerton and moved to bigger premises in Bath. I went with it, but I didn't like the driving. We'd bought a house in Glastonbury and soon enough I was driving to work. It was 27 miles to Bath, all winding hills and 30mph villages, but pretty soon I was on a five-day week and then I was working just as hard as I had been in London and this didn't go down well in the context of the fact that we'd moved to the West Country for a new life. Eventually I moved out of the family home into a flat in Bath.

Once again I'd been caught up in the whirl of a technological revolution. There were more magazines, more designers, more journalists, more advertising people and increasing amounts of management to contend with. Chris proved just as adept at keeping the show on the road as Lee had done, but in a more promising industry which replaced the logistics of shifting computer software tapes around the country with publishing a new wave of computer games magazines to a whole new market of geeks who were finally finding a culture which reflected back at them what they most wanted to see: stuff.

Chris, who went on to make the TED workshops a huge global phenomenon, turned out to be ahead of the game every which way, always launching new titles and coming up with new ideas like giving away free software CDs with games and tools on the cover. He never made a professional mistake all the time I worked for him and his success provided livelihoods for hundreds of people over many decades. He worked quickly and trusted the team around him. He was charming, erudite and incredibly genial.

One day, on a Monday morning in 1988, we arrived at the office to find new Apple Macs on every desk. No one knew they were due, nor was there any training involved. The software was version 1.1 of Quark XPress, which became the industry standard for 20 years.

"So what are we getting in terms of training?" I asked him.

"It's okay," said Chris, "just switch it on and take it from there, it's self-explanatory. I'll come round and talk you through any problems, but Macs are very easy to use."

Indeed they were: in fact they were a dream come true, and opened up a new era of publishing in which the writer could control the way his or her copy looked on the printed page. The freedom of expression that the new technology brought with it was euphoric. Suddenly we could define not just what we wrote, but how it looked on the printed page. I gave no thought to those who would be put out of work because of the new technology: I had no roots in journalism, my background was as an entrepreneur in the computer games sector. Computers meant a new golden age for some, it involved a change of trade for others. The job losses meant the traditional typesetting cadre, for instance, were suddenly redundant.

Peak readership – and employment – for newspapers in the UK was, as was mentioned earlier, in the mid-1950s. There were all sorts of separate skill sets. Until the mid-80s, writing for the paper was one job, and producing it was another. The production process involved several different skills, each performed by a different worker, and now they were all condensed into one person at a computer rather than half a dozen scattered across the premises. With the arrival of the first Apple Macs in the UK, there was a fork in the road: some people would take the publishing sector onwards, while others – the typesetters and machinists of the outgoing technology – would find their services no longer required. Computers ushered in changes similar to the arrival of the Gutenberg Press, and we were being press-ganged into it. The quill was amplified by hot metal, then by electricity.

By the late 1980s it was clear that what had been a cottage industry was morphing into a vast global computer revolution and PCs – personal computers – were becoming consumer goods. Offices began installing the new machines to do word processing and accounts. Staff were trained to use the new equipment, and improvements and upgrades started arriving on a regular basis.

I can't honestly say I was too bothered by the loss of the old techniques. It might be easy to look back, dewy-eyed, now, but the pre-computer production process was extremely laborious and then it became extremely efficient. I didn't have enough experience in the trade to have made friends across the industry. I didn't have to bid farewell to any close colleagues, not at that time anyway.

– Chapter 4 –

Soon after moving to Bath Chris made himself chairman and brought in a new managing director and the new boss was none other than Greg Ingham, who had been my deputy at *CTW*. The reversal of fortune unsettled me, and I felt awkward about it. There was no bad blood with Greg, but I wanted to put the past behind me and that meant I didn't appreciate it being touted in my face every day. Suddenly work wasn't so much fun any more and the enjoyment began to drain away from my job.

Reservations about whether the computer games industry was contributing to the good of humanity also rose to the surface at around this time. Games that involved death and destruction were the biggest sellers. It was dispiriting. It was a make-believe world: why was everyone escaping from the actual world, was it really so bad? And if you did want escapism, why escape into war?

Computer users were getting younger and everyone was spending increasing amounts of time glued to a screen. It didn't seem healthy to the point that I no longer really wanted to be a part of it. It seemed infantile to be selling teenagers the means to stunt their emotional and perhaps intellectual progress, and as toxic as selling them hard drugs.

At the same time Jo wanted me to be around more, and eventually I moved back to Glastonbury.

I no longer loved the industry I'd helped birth when I left Bath, my flat and Future Publishing in early 1989. It was tough to say goodbye to Chris but I knew I'd be a liability if I stayed – my heart wasn't in it any more. In fact I decided I was doing him a favour, and I needed a favour from him in return, so I arranged to have a chat and explained that my circumstances had changed, I was no longer able to give 100 per cent, and it was time for me to go.

Chris said he was sorry to hear that, and asked whether there anything he could do to help.

"Yes," I said, "you could sack me: that way I'll be able to claim benefits straight away because I don't have any reserves to fall back on at this stage."

"OK," said Chris, "if you're sure that's what you want, that's okay with me."

It was a bittersweet moment. Until then my star had been rising, more or less. I'd been there at the start of a new industry. I'd helped forge a path at the start of the computer era, and surprised and delighted friends and family who'd supposed I was wasting my time. I had an intimate knowledge of how the whole phenomenon had originated in the early 80s, but now I could make no more use of it: my future lay elsewhere. I'd turned 30 and it was time to do something else, but I didn't know what. Little did I know that I would be living on government benefits for more than seven years before I finally worked it out.

I decided to go back to live in Glastonbury, and rented a room in a shared house which belonged to the town's Osho community.

The Osho house was a good base. I've always loved Osho – or Bhagwan Shree Rajneesh as he was originally – even from before going to India. His discourses and books on psychology and religious history are just incredible – incisive, witty and beautifully structured. Whether it's Islam,

Hinduism, Taoism, Christianity or Judaism, he's fluent in the culture he's talking about. He seemed to understand the Christian tradition from the inside out. This ability to switch from his own background – Hinduism – into another sensibility appealed to me as someone whose father was a Jew and mother a Christian. I was – am – the son of an immigrant and felt duty-bound to investigate my inherited narratives before handing them on. Anyone from a mixed heritage will understand that imperative, though of course, it's complicated.

My mother's story was very English: she was born into an upper middle class family in Ewell, Surrey. The family owned Butterworths, England's leading law publisher. The firm had been acquired by my great-grandfather, Charles Bond, but when the time came my grandfather, Charles Shaw Bond, the eldest son, chose not to take it on. He was an optical doctor at Moorfields Eye Hospital, and wanted to continue his service, so the running of the firm was delegated to his younger brother, Stanley Bond, who ran the firm with great success from when he took it on in 1895 until his death in 1943, at which point the firm was put into a trust (you can read about this in a book called *From Trust to Takeover: Butterworths 1938-1968, A Publishing House in Transition* by Gordon Graham). Butterworths was bought in 1967 by Reed and continues to be managed by Reed Elsevier.

Charles Shaw Bond, my grandfather, had five children – two daughters and three sons – with his vivacious Australian wife Eleanor. In order of birth they were Marjorie, Kenneth, Joan (my mum), Ron and Gerald. All served in the armed forces during the Second World War and returned alive.

Their postings included Egypt and Iran for uncle Ken, Burma for uncle Gerald, Europe for uncle Ron, Scotland – a Wren's posting – for aunt Marjie and Uxbridge for mum, who was in the WAAF, the Women's Auxiliary Air Force. They all came home with incredible stories and hardly a scratch between them but, sadly, Eleanor died in an electrical accident in the family garden during the war. A bomb had caused live wires to become exposed and she accidentally stood on one: my grandfather, who was some 20 years older, didn't last long without her and was also gone by the time my elder sister Julia was born in 1957.

There was a sense in the family that we had been deprived of great riches which had gone to others, which may or may not have been true, since not everyone can be a business genius in the Stanley Bond mould. But what can be said is that it was a bold decision by my grandfather: he recognised that inheriting a business he had no interest in was probably not in the best interests of either himself or the business' employees. And yet the result was perhaps more modest lives for his children than might have otherwise have been the case. On such matters are fates decided. My mother always reminded us – myself and my two sisters, Julie and Frances – that selflessness is a virtue, and that giving to others is both an honour and a duty and, in my grandfather's case, a calling, which has precedence over fame and fortune. And so, in my family, there is a precedent.

My father, meanwhile, was born in Cairo in the 1920s, the son of an Italian cotton trader who went to live in Egypt and export cotton rather than stay in Italy and import cotton. I'm the only son of a first-generation immigrant and having an exotic surname required me to explain my origins on countless occasions from the age of about eight. I don't qualify as Jewish, because Judaism is a matriarchal religion and my mother was Christian, but people assume I am, which is probably fair enough, but it's a complicated story to explain on the phone or at the door and even today, when it's too much of a chore to disabuse them of the notion that I'm of Yiddish extraction, I just don't bother and go along with it. It certainly helps when it's the Jehovah's Witnesses calling.

Other than that there's very little to go on: my father had left Egypt without any photographs or mementos of his family, and his father and mother had both passed on before he left. None of his family or network went to the UK, they scattered to the US, France, Peru and Switzerland. His brother Elie, who my sisters and I never met, migrated to Quebec in Canada where he became a teacher. My dad just wasn't very keen to share much of his backstory with me or indeed anyone. It hadn't helped that in Egypt he had been wealthy, and all his money was sequestered by the Egyptian state and he had to start over. He did okay, got a PhD in Philosophy and worked for the government's developing countries trade department. Later in life he resumed his Jewish identity which he appeared to have put to one side for many decades. Curiously, and in very different circumstances, both my mother and father had servants as children. Those were different times, I guess.

If my dad was monosyllabic about his past, a lot of people who lived through the war years were like that too. They just wanted to forget about it and move on. People develop the narrative threads of their lives by sharing anecdotes, but I'd stopped asking my father any questions by my mid-teens. Unexpectedly, however, in the Osho house in Glastonbury I began to appreciate how deeply Jewish culture informed my view of the world, and started to value the intellectual flexibility it offered. Community, for Jewish people, seemed to be a petri dish from which lots of interesting creativity could emerge. But I still couldn't find a way to belong: I remained a religious nomad in all but name, and even that wasn't very convincing.

A long time was spent listening to Leonard Cohen's music and tried to tease out the Talmudic lessons the songs seemed to be imparting – slightly odd behaviour while residing in what was essentially a mini-commune based around the teachings of a new age guru, but the Osho school of life is nothing if not generous and at no point was I made to feel alienated or unwelcome. It felt fantastic to connect with the songs, and the Talmudic teachings they imparted. Having been raised as a Church of England Christian, New Testament stories were very familiar from church and school. Religious studies then included no religious teaching other than Christianity. However, it always seemed that most Old Testament stories, from the Garden of Eden onwards, were very questionable. The New Testament seemed to have more rounded characters in it, and we were given to understand the parables and stories were of crucial significance to our lives in ways, albeit in ways which were never properly explained.

The parable of the mustard seed, for instance: a small seed with many gifts. So where were the mustard seeds in my life, and which were the important ones? Was it the seed of laughter, or the seed of forgiveness, or of redemption, or living a good life, or of bravado, or penitence? All of them? Consider a saying such as "man shall not live by bread alone". OK, so what was on offer – this wasn't dietary advice, surely? It referred to the spiritual odyssey of course, but how was one to chart one's life for a spiritual journey? Too often, the Protestant path seemed very faint, and when it trailed away I felt obliged to look for answers elsewhere.

The Osho community lasted but a few months when the owner of the house was suddenly and outrageously killed on Hampstead Heath in London. He was out jogging listening to his Walkman (the Sony Walkman was a cassette-based early version of Apple's iPod) when a motorcyclist – on the Heath illegally – rode into him at speed and he died instantly.

The effect was cathartic: the upshot was that the Glastonbury Osho house was to be sold and the tenants obliged to leave. I had nowhere to go, but I did co-own a house in town, and eventually I asked Jo if I could move into the garden. I said I would build a shed far from the house, on the side of Chalice Hill, and live in that. The idea had occurred some time before when I was reading about the life of the famous psychotherapist and anthropologist Carl Gustav Jung, who had built himself a hut in the grounds of his home in Switzerland and lived and worked in it with great success. He noted that a new space had no previous residual pathologies trapped in it, the absence of which, he said, conveyed a certain liberty to whomsoever dwelled therein. It interested me that someone apparently so cerebral built his own home. To my surprise Jo agreed and thus began the move into the garden.

The building work began at the start of one of the hottest summers on record. Getting the materials on to Chalice Hill proved exhausting, and the process took two or three weeks, but eventually I'd created a room with a plastic corrugated roof and a couple of windows and a door (found at house clearances and builder's merchants).

One morning, when I woke and went down the hill to the house to make tea in the kitchen, I found Emily and Florence playing and no sign of their mother. After a few days as the lone carer, I realised I was becoming a single parent with two young children to feed and look after.

– Chapter 5 –

The astrology magazine, *New Astrologer*, that Jo and I had started when we became interested in astrology, had briefly looked promising but eventually proved too big an ask and was sold. Along the way, however, I'd gotten immersed in Glastonbury lore and started writing a book, called *AD: The One That Got Away*, an updated take on the legend of Joseph of Arimathea set in Avalon, the sacred island featured in the Arthurian legend.

Joseph was said to have been Jesus' uncle – it was reportedly his burial chamber that Jesus was laid in before his ascension – and, following the crucifixion, he allegedly left the Holy Land, saying that he would take a staff and wherever he planted the staff would be the centre of a new church. The legend is that the staff was planted in Glastonbury, on a hill called Wearyall Hill, where a Holy Thorn tree duly grew. A cutting of this tree now grows in St John's Church on the High Street, and a sprig is sent to the Royal household every Christmas. The book, *AD*, proved to be slow to write, not least because it was a historical novel and accuracy was important. It wasn't until much later, when George RR Martin came up with *Game of Thrones,* that I realised that the narrative – the story – is everything: no one cares how much iron goes into a sword or precisely how long it takes to shoe a horse. It was a decade before that book was finished, and by then the fun had long gone out of it. But I learned a lot along the way.

Being single parent is a full-time role, but pin money was needed. Doing astrology readings was a favourite, and thanks to the new astrology software becoming available I could do the calculations for a chart by computer rather than by hand. I also read tarot cards using the Mythic Tarot deck, which used the Greek myths as their storylines – Jason and the Golden Fleece was one theme, another was the tale of Psyche and Eros. I enjoyed developing these skills: having studied psychology, it felt like an outlet for some of the knowledge I'd acquired. With computer software these very old disciplines could be rediscovered for a modern age – and the work could be done after the children went to bed. Sometimes I hooked up with chums to do tarot readings at Psychic Fairs around the West Country.

By the early 1990s there was a reconciliation with Jo, and Charlie was born in November 1991, but we maintained separate homes. Me and the girls moved into a house on Windmill Hill, an estate at the top of a small hill to the north of Glastonbury. Charlie lived with his mum in her flat in Street. After a while she embarked on a new relationship from which she was to bear a fourth child, Agate, or Aggie as she became known.

For the first two years of his life, I saw very little of Charlie. Then, one night, I was lying in bed at 2 in the morning and couldn't sleep. I kept thinking "something's going on". Then there was a knock at the door. I answered: it was a policewoman, with a male colleague.

"We've heard you may be the father of a young boy," she said. "His mother's been detained and we were going to take him into care, but if you are the father and want to have custody then you have that option."

"Bring him in," I said. Charlie looked very bedraggled but slept very well after a bit of fussing. In a way I was elated: the thought of repeating the dynamic I had with my father with my own son terrified me, and now at least I would have a chance to connect and even nurture the laddie.

But clearly what had started out as post-natal depression had become much more serious. Jo was taken away and sectioned – detained in an institution under the 1983 Mental Health Act. There were lots more sections to come before she was diagnosed as bi-polar.

By the mid-1990s I started to consider leaving the West Country. There was actually a moment when it was apparent our time in Glastonbury was ending: a dear friend and counsel, Bahli, came over for coffee and a chat one morning, and as she was leaving I heard a voice, just like the voice I'd heard on my first visit to Glastonbury, which said: "When Bahli leaves the house, your time in Glastonbury will be up." I don't know why it happened like that: I could have delayed her departure by asking her if she wanted another cup of tea, but it would only have postponed the inevitable. Bahli was a wonderful companion on the path for many years, and it was a wrench to leave her and many other friends though some, like Jaine and Andy, are life-long companions. Bahli was too, but she passed on early, ever the spirit flower.

Apart from the sense of having reached a dead end in Somerset, I wanted to be closer to my wonderful mum Joan and still incomprehensibly foreign dad, David, in their later years. And I wanted a job. I wanted our kids to have a chance of a decent lifestyle which was unlikely where we were. And even though we were divorced, I wanted to leave with Jo, however impossible that seemed. This was partly because she was the kids' mum, partly because there was a chance that being away from Glastonbury would help resolve her mental health issues, and partly because there was no one I wanted to be with more.

Unbeknownst to me, however, the relationship with Aggie's father was not going well, and Jo suggested that she and Aggie could move with us. I accepted of course, and the die was cast.

In the mid-80s Glastonbury had enjoyed a renaissance as a sort of new age community with a profound connection to the legend of Avalon. One day in 1987 the town had been the focal point for the Harmonic Convergence, an event in the Mayan calendar which signals the start of a new era for humanity. There were all sorts of global travellers tramping past our house for many weeks, from California, Australia, New Zealand and across the United Kingdom and Europe. It was a high point of the global village in action, but nine years later it was a different story: the potential of the moment seemed to have passed. Too many relationships and communities proved transient, and new teachings hadn't taken deep enough root and were being all but swept away by drugs like heroin and two new drugs, ecstasy and crack cocaine. Suddenly it didn't feel like too a good place to raise children any more. There would be other cycles, I knew – Glastonbury is a wonderful place graced with pre-historic mystery – but this one was over.

The process of moving involved swapping the council-owned house we lived in for another council-owned house on a list held at the council offices. There were hundreds of houses from around the country on the list: after a process of some months we settled on a property in Cambridge.

Neither of us had much of a connection with Cambridge, but my grandfather had been a Cambridge Blue and it was close enough to my parents' north London home to go there and back in a day, so off we went, arriving in September 1996, once more with an unknown and indeed uncertain future awaiting us.

– Chapter 6 –

After a couple of weeks of settling in to Cambridge, it was time to start looking for work. There were a few concerns: mainly a seven-year gap on my CV. Tricky. What with one thing and another I'd never actually had a job interview – ever. It was always a phone call and it had gone from there, so I wasn't quite sure how to explain the gap if it came to an interview situation.

This still being the pre-internet age – Tim Berners-Lee had invented the world wide web in 1990, but it didn't really catch on until much later in the 1990s – I went to the nearest shop and bought the local paper. On the way back from the shop I opened the paper to check out the jobs section and immediately it occurred to me: why not ring the paper and find out if they needed anyone? After all, I had both production and writing experience. Surely that could be a valuable combination? At that time – and it still holds true as I write this – there was no formal qualification for being a sub-editor, other than an ability to do the job. Because there was no conventional route into the job, you had to have your wits about you to make a go of it, and that was fine by me. It also made for some interesting companions – others who liked, or were obliged, to live by their wits.

I rang the number listed on the masthead and asked to speak to the chief sub-editor, and was put through to Nigel Brookes, who asked me if I could sub. I said yes and he explained they were a man down after one of the subs had been signed off sick for a few weeks and could I come in on Thursday? I said yes.

I showed up on the Thursday and was led through an old building which can only be called Dickensian. It was gloomy and oppressive, with big ceilings and high windows. The old print works were still there, and there were typesetters and ink-based crews all the way to the newsroom. The whole place smelt of ink and metal. The dress code was suits and ties for men and smart outfits for women. Mentally the clock turned back in my head, to my first job as a journalist in 1985. The technology was a typewriter, a telephone and a notebook/pen. Within a couple of years I had an Apple Mac on my desk, but the days of shiny new Apple Macs to play with seemed very far away from the *Cambridge Evening News*. As I walked to the newsroom it felt like I'd seen the future and now I was being transported back to the past where a nasty headache awaited me.

The site on the Newmarket Road had been home to the much-respected paper for decades. The title had been published every day of the week except Sundays since 1888. The owners – the Iliffe family – had originally bought the title in the 1920s, sold it in 1938, and then reacquired it in 1959. Lord Iliffe was a wealthy man with a spread of interests in property, TV and print.

I got to a desk and was shown how to use an old green-screen computer, all too like the Commodore Pet I'd encountered in Manchester nearly 20 years previously. There was no email or internet. I wasn't even high enough up the food chain to have my own phone. I knew I had to settle down and put in a proper shift, come what may, at least for a couple of years, but it took a huge amount of self-control not to just swivel and walk right back out the door and find the quickest route out of town on the nearest hobbit express.

So began my stint as a news sub-editor at the *Cambridge Evening News*. Little did I know it, but during my time at the paper the introduction of new technology into everyday working life would affect every aspect of economic and cultural endeavour, with colossal consequences for the publishing industry, and indeed the way the economy – locally, nationally and globally – operates.

– Chapter 7 –

Ten years in Somerset had taught me one thing I'd never fully appreciated before: people and the relationships you develop are pivotal in every aspect of life. I'd met a lot of folks who'd been pretty crazy in the computer games industry, people driven by all sorts of inner urgings, some with the brains of mobsters, others with the morals of psychopaths. It didn't really matter too much about any of that, though, I'd concluded: what mattered was your personal chemistry with other people. Sometimes the ones with the sickest minds or saddest hearts were the most interesting but whatever, if you've got chemistry then you'll find common ground. You have to find a way to make your relationships work and I figured if I was going to be stuck in this subterranean newspaper world for a while, there'd hopefully be some interesting companions, even if I had to bide my time to work out who they might be.

I certainly couldn't afford to make any mistakes. The mistakes I'd made in the past had been expensive in all sorts of ways: I was like a cat who'd already used up a fair few of its nine lives, and now I'd have to be much more circumspect. But fortunately it wasn't too long before my hope proved correct.

The subs desk was my habitat. I started off as a down-table sub in a team of 16, give or take a couple of casuals. I was near the lowest rung in the office: below me were copy editors, who copied letters into the new word processing software, and below them were copy runners, who took messages between departments and between us and the print works. This was how it was before email started breaking up these finely nuanced roles. Copy runners, for instance, went right back to the days when runners would take orders from the generals to the front line, and return with reports of battlefield action. The role actually goes right back to the ancient Greeks, when a runner called Pheidippides ran the 26 miles from Marathon to Athens to deliver news of a military victory against the Persians at the battle of Marathon. Then he died of exhaustion, but that was probably because he'd done a similar run a few days before, except that one had been 140 miles and took three days. Copy runners had a great backstory. One of the last ones at the *News* was our eldest, Emily, who held the position for a while in her teens. Put her off work for years.

Anyway it turned out that my immediate boss, the chief sub-editor Nigel Brookes, was good at his job. The department was well run and had some very talented people on board – men and women. The industry was quite healthy in respect of gender, I noticed, certainly far healthier than the computer games industry, which was dominated by geek males, so in that sense at least it was progress.

The *Cambridge Evening News* was selling about 48,000 copies a day in the mid-1990s, which was pretty good going. Cambridge then was a city of around 110,000 residents, but the circulation area extending north to Ely and Wisbech, south to Royston and Saffron Walden, east to Newmarket and Bury St Edmunds, and west to Huntingdon and even a corner of Bedfordshire. What was the *Cambridge Evening News* in Cambridge was rejigged as the *Newmarket Evening News* for

Newmarket, the *Huntingdon Evening News, Royston Evening News* and so on for each other large town in the vicinity. It was the same paper but had a different front page with stories about that town on it. It was a lot of work to produce all these copies.

There were precious few competitors. The paper virtually had a monopoly. There were a couple of weekly papers for nearby local towns: the *Hunts Post* and the *Newmarket Journal* among them. But they were tiny outposts compared to the hub that was Cambridge. Maybe, because there were no obvious competitors, the management was lulled into thinking they had it all tied up: there's no shame in that, since everyone else was too busy in the soap opera of the industry to consider that the arrival of the internet might bring a threat. The notion that the digital world might host news content had probably not even occurred to Tim Berners-Lee, who invented the world wide web, though it probably crossed Steve Jobs' mind at some point. This was the quiet before the storm, though we didn't know it.

The editor was an old-school headmaster type, Robert Satchwell, who ran the paper with an iron, but fair, will. At that point the editor of a newspaper was the most important man in the firm other than the managing director, who wasn't on site every day. While the managing director's office was set away from the factory floor, the editor's was centre stage. No one would cross the editor: the decisions he made were law. If you said that within 15 years a newspaper editor would become the puppet of shareholders, there simply to transmit the desires and whims of the market to staff... well, you would have been laughed out of the newsroom. The power flowed from the editor outwards: he was at the epicentre of the matrix. There was no other model for newspapers, regional or national.

If the paper's ethos was transmitted from the editor's office, and Satchwell was old school, it was only to be expected that he had old school henchmen. Peter Wells was the deputy editor and he was a man to be reckoned with. He had a fierce way about him and wasn't afraid of taking down anyone who tried to step into his path. Peter and Nigel were the enforcers. All organisations have them, to keep the unruly masses in line, and these were the days before Human Resources (HR) departments became the law-givers and newsrooms became more collegiate. These crew-masters kept the team in check in time-honoured fashion: by appearing reasonable while retaining the capacity to inspire fear. That was just how things were and you knew you had to keep out of their way as much as possible. I hadn't encountered enforcers in the workplace before, such had been my gilded career, but I knew what the job entailed from boarding school days. I just had to get on with my job and keep my nose clean.

Other than that there was little to go on. The work was demanding and intense, and the technology basic. We didn't have email in 1996, let alone the internet. My colleagues thought the technology was a bit beyond me, but actually it was a bit behind me. Everything had been so much fun on Apple Macs. If I wanted a headline I just drew a box on the page, picked a font and point size, and keyed the headline straight in. But the *News*' system at the end of the 20th century involved a written description of the headline – you couldn't see the full page onscreen. You just had text, no boxes, and you wrote the headline out in a clumsy code which looked something like:

H 60, F10, D3: <Diana dies/in Paris/car crash>
This describes a 60 point headline (large) with ten characters on three decks (rows). You sent your headline over to the design team who laid it out on the page and brought back a proof to read. If you wanted it changed, you had to write the correction on the proof and send it back to the design team. It was all incredibly tedious and time-consuming, though soon enough we got the technology to print out our own proofs, which made the job easier, or at least quicker. I didn't mind: I was lucky to have gotten in the door and extremely fortunate that no one had asked me for my CV. I just wanted to remain anonymous and work hard. Lord Iliffe was my saviour, little did he know it.

After a few days one of the subs, Ian Walker, invited me to join him for a drink at the Rose & Crown a couple of hundred yards away from the office. It was an incredibly dingy and badly lit pub, full of smoke and working men (the smoking ban in UK pubs came into force on July 1, 2007). A couple of hours later, I was leaving and asked Ian if he was okay to get home. He explained that he had an armchair in a room upstairs when he got too drunk, and he would sleep there. It seemed incredibly depressing. I'd never heard of such behaviour and I'd frequented some pretty full-on pubs in Manchester, London and Somerset. Pubs are always a bit of a soap opera, but this was a whole other level: uncomfortable, a bit pathetic and resolutely unattractive. I said cheerio and never went back to the Rose & Crown again. I badly missed my friends in Somerset and wondered if we'd done the right thing by moving. The only good thing about Cambridge at that point was that the kids were in good schools – St Bede's and Abbey Meadows – and we had a nice, if sparsely furnished, home.

Most of the other subs lived out of town and were therefore not really eligible as drinking partners. One of the few that seemed friendly was a senior by the name of Mark Swift. Mark was a South African poet who had come to England when the apartheid regime became too monstrous for his sensibilities. He was extremely likeable and seemed to see me as a curio, perhaps worthy of further examination. Neither of us was to know that the bond forged in this unlikely setting would result in his son, his ex-wife, his son's ex-partner and their children becoming part of an extended and very loving family – a family based on bonds of loyalty, friendship and love, rather than blood.

"Watch out for him, he's two-faced," Mark said of a senior reporter as I crossed the newsroom floor one time. It was a first glimpse into the internal dynamics of the newsroom. The Newmarket Road was home to 42 reporters and along with 16 sub-editors, four full-on features writers plus two doing TV and features, three copy typists, six on sport, two editorial copy runners, a deputy editor, picture editor, features editor, business editor, production editor and the editor… " it was a helluva editorial staff", as sports sub-editor and magazine designer Andrew Ormiston said many years later. And that list doesn't include the teams on the weekly titles, which added another 40 or 50 folks to the roster.

The *Cambridge Evening News* was then a significant local employer about whom I knew almost nothing, and Mark's comment suggested another layer of communality which could be explored. It turned out he lived in the most bohemian part of Cambridge, on Gwydir Street, and I became a sometime visitor. He delighted in sharing stories about his past, about South Africa, about literature, about his family, and he was very good company, with a sharp sense of the absurd and beautifully cultivated manners. But there was something "other" about him which I never fully appreciated until much later, when I was foundering on the rocks of crisis, and recognised in him the nobility of suffering which is apparent in myths and legends – and, yes, history – yet frequently misunderstood, and he tried to understand it, the road less travelled. He was a poet who left his homeland and had suffered in ways that I could barely comprehend but, most of all, he was brilliant company.

The self-eviction from a homeland I could understand: we had left the much-loved West Country for economic reasons. But Mark… why had he left his homeland? For fame and fortune, for glory? That didn't seem plausible, and the enigma remained: a published poet and writer who had reworked his trade so that his role now was to tinker with the efforts of others who could never aspire to the heights he had already laid claim to. Why – was it a cruel streak of the muse's, or was he learning something of significance that had been omitted in his earlier life? Had he done this as a choice, or had he arrived in Cambridge thinking that great literary prizes awaited him, and what happened was he became a sub on the local paper? Mark had the angelically roué looks of a young

Martin Amis, the novelist who captivated a generation in Britain in the 1980s, and he combined that with a ferocious Afrikaans humour. One time he'd been in an interview on BBC radio and all his answers were in Afrikaans, much to the bewilderment of the interviewer.

For some reason he took me under his wing and I learned a lot about writing from him. I was still writing *AD*, and I knew there was something missing in my authorial armoury. Clues were what I was looking for, and Mark had plenty of them. "Writing is like standing on a stone," he said one evening over another bottle of wine. "You want to cross the river but you can't think about that because you've got to get to the next stone first. You have to be sure of your footing to get across: take one step at a time. The next step is all that matters." That was sagacity speaking. Through my work as a sub a renewed realisation of how crucial it is to read through one's writing and edit and re-edit it was instilled in me, and oh how careful you have to be to get to the next stone without slipping!

"You can't worry about the destination, you just have to concentrate on the next stone."

The subs desk was a riotous assembly of characters who performed like Trojans when it mattered and chilled out the rest of the time. Thanks to their dedication and skill, an amazing paper – or series of papers – was crafted every day. There was Les, who appeared to have decided that his companions were all mad and needed to be treated like wayward children. And Don, who reminded me that this was Viking country, and I had come from the more poetic world of the Celts, far out west where the Romans had no friends and words were the shapers of destiny rather than swords. Don was a bit of a gangster, but in a good way: if you were trusted, he would look after you. And Keith, who had the driest sense of humour, and a mind so sharp that if you used even one lazy word in a headline, he would mock you all week.

There was M-J – Mary-Jane – who'd spent a lot of time in Russia and had no time for fools. And John Meredith, a lovely man and first-class musician, able to see humour in every exchange. The subs desk was full of wits like John and Barry Peters – acerbic, sardonic, and impossible not to like. Plus Jane, whose humour was cheeky and reminded me of a Glastonbury pixie, and quiet Graham Turner who never gave anything away… And there was Phil, the deputy chief sub, trying to hold it together and retain some authority. It was maverick central, as befitted a group of people who had all taken the road less travelled to get where they were. To that extent at least, Mark was one among equals.

By and by, it felt like being among comrades, and I got to hear their stories, which were mainly drinking tales. One of the subs, Mike Hills, went into a local pub for a beer and got chatting to some US Air Force types. After the pub closed they invited him back to their place, so he went along to the Lakenheath with them, but while he was there, there was a security alert and the site was in shutdown mode for three days. This being in the analogue days before mobile phones, Mrs Hills was apparently in a bit of a state when he finally got home. All innocent enough, and if the drink got the better of you the company looked after you really well. Or just turned a blind eye.

– Chapter 8 –

Things were changing at the *Cambridge Evening News* in the mid-1990s: a new print works and office was being built on the outskirts of town and the newsroom was due to move into it in early 1997.

The site we were on had been sold to a developer: prices for city-centre property were starting to skyrocket and parking in town was becoming impractical. Moving out of the centre of towns wasn't a strategy only being pursued in Cambridge, it was the norm at this time. It was a double whammy: you got the money from selling up, and the facilities on the edge of town were a lot cheaper. And of course these sell-offs worked in the short term but, by moving away from their own bases – the places where their readers lived and worked – newspapers were voluntarily loosening their connection with the community they were supposed to be serving, and that would have consequences. Maybe they hoped it wouldn't matter, and readers wouldn't notice. The business logic certainly stacked up.

There was no immediate blowback following these moves. It was unusual for a town to have two regional newspapers in it, so in general if a firm moved out further afield no one would move on to the just-vacated patch, and there was no danger of losing market share to competitors. The notion that the internet would initiate a virtual patch and readers might migrate to that instead wasn't on anyone's radar. If it had been, would these papers have stayed closer to their readers? It's hard to say but the point is that strategies had a blind spot about where the technology might be leading and blind spots make it difficult to position your business for future economic environments. However, no one knew what was going to happen next, probably not even Steve Jobs, who had been in the wilderness from 1985 until he rejoined Apple in 1997 and even then, after he took back the helm, it would be another ten years before the first iPhone was released. No one predicted the winners and losers of the internet. It would like predicting which countries would benefit from the invention of football.

Revolutions take time to brew, and then they reach a critical mass and it looks as though it's happened overnight. The changing of the guard is not an exact science. As Bill Gates said: "We always overestimate the change that will occur in the next two years and underestimate the change that will occur in the next ten. Don't let yourself be lulled into inaction."

But gradually, during the 20th century, a religion-based society was being replaced by a secular society, powerfully enabled by new portals of technology. The analogue age was being making way for the digital age, though we couldn't see the full picture – wouldn't have recognised it if we had seen it in the same way as horse riders would never have guessed what a car might look like, or how it would change things. You can't blame that on the newspaper trade, of course, because consumers are fickle, but what we did know was that the move to Milton was a sea change and after the implications sank in it became clear that not everyone would work at the new base.

One of the ones who wouldn't make it was Heather Nunn, the tea lady, who came round with a tea trolley twice a day. Heather was well into her fifties at least, and was wonderfully coarse. She made tea and instant coffee – making coffee with freshly ground beans was still unusual in the UK in the 1990s – and served sandwiches and cakes. You really didn't want to think about how the sandwiches were made: I avoided buying them. While you waited for your tea she would say something like: "Ooh, yes, that's freshly squeezed, that milk is, and you can pull the udder one if you like!" Or, while handing you a slice of cake: "Don't worry, I changed my knickers a week ago, love, you've got nothing to worry about." She was a classic character in a firm full of characters, and she was the first to go.

Just weeks after moving into the new building, there was an incident which heralded the changing of the guard. A young female reporter complained about the way she was treated by her managers on the newsroom floor, and the complaint couldn't be brushed under the carpet, so a company meeting was called in the conference room of the new building.

The subject was bullying in the newsroom. Apparently this had been going on for years, it was said to be institutionalised, at least among the reporters. I didn't notice anything going on with the subs den though. It was firm, it was harsh sometimes, but it was fair enough in the context of a whole lot of work needed to get done and you couldn't carry anyone: everyone had to stand up and be counted – or rather, sit down and be counted.

It's helps to differentiate what bullying is and what's just "the system". My own experiences were formed at boarding school. For instance, as junior boarders we were obliged to go on runs every week. There was a prefect at the front but bringing up the rear was another senior who wasn't a prefect. He carried a hockey stick and he would thwack the last boy among maybe 20 runners on the back of the legs, or on the ankles. It bloody hurt and it messed with your head as well as the rhythm of your run. Yes it was sadistic, vicious and twisted, but you couldn't fool yourself into thinking it was bullying, because it wasn't. On one level it was entirely impersonal. The pupil thwacking juniors at the back of a run didn't care who the person was: his job was to get everyone to run faster. Bullying isn't like that. Bullying is directed at an individual, and it's personal. It's directed at your defects, your weaknesses, or your intelligence, your clothes, hair, walk, or weight – anything that could be used to undermine you as a human being, to belittle you.

What was happening at the *Cambridge Evening News* wasn't actual bullying, it was more like institutionalised psychological aggression, released in inappropriate ways. That doesn't make it any better, or excuse it, but it was impersonal. No one teased you to the point that you broke down – or maybe they did and I just didn't see it. Apparently new reporters – most often female reporters – were on occasion humiliated, "picked on", their copy torn apart, their motives and abilities questioned, and the rest of it. I didn't know what to think, but if you asked me if I saw any of it, I'd have to say I didn't, but I was on the sub's desk, and the reporters desk was almost completely foreign to me. I had no inside personal contacts or pals there.

Anyway, the appointed hour of the company meeting came and 120 people from the advertising, editorial, distribution and accounts/personnel departments trooped over to the conference theatre in the main print hall, where senior management awaited them.

We walked in and sat down in silence. The editor stood to one side while the managing director read out a prepared statement to the effect that there had been allegations of mistreatment in the workplace and any instance of demeaning or provocative behaviour would not be tolerated in any way. A protocol was to be established so that any member of staff could initiate a complaint – which, bizarrely, would initially be handled by the line manager, who could be the source of the issue – and, if they were not happy with the way the complaint was handled, they could escalate their concerns until they were fully and properly addressed.

The theme of the meeting was that this alleged workplace bullying was taking place between members of staff who were of equal status, and indeed it is entirely plausible that this was what they thought the problem was. It may have been that no one wanted to draw the senior management's attention to any dynamic other than reporter-on-reporter incidents. To an outsider it might seem that the meeting was called to address just this problem, and perhaps it had been – because that's all they'd been told about.

It was a very interesting moment in the company's history. As the spectacle unfolded, the process itself became the focus: would there be an opportunity to take questions from the floor and, if so, would anyone dare to spell out the nature of some of these more troubling newsroom dynamics?

After an extensive preamble the floor was handed over to the editor to explain how the protocol would work. Mr Satchwell was businesslike and professional. He knew nothing about any bullying in his newsroom, and was horrified at the suggestion that such proclivities might be possible. When he invited questions from the floor it was clear he wanted only specific questions about how the protocol would work. The first couple of questions addressed the protocol, and how much privacy the complainant would have. Everyone knew that if someone broke line and reported on anyone else in their team they would be seen as a snitch, and that might complicate their prospects of happiness at the firm.

Finally a sub raised his hand. It was the last question. Keith Bailey posed a meandering analysis which seemed to be going nowhere, but just at the end of it he made the point that everyone was waiting for.

"So would you say," Keith said from the floor, "that any of the possible bullying described in your statement this afternoon could possibly be bullying of juniors by staff with longer service, and is that is being overlooked by management?"

There was a crystal silence. All eyes turned to Robert Satchwell. He tried to go back over the protocol, he insisted that any incidents would be taken seriously, he... something funny was happening. He seemed to be going through profound mental contortions to find the right formula of words, a formula to answer the question without admitting to or denying the central charge. After a couple of minutes, he'd failed to find the right words, and then he had no words left. He seemed to have lost two stone. No one else on the podium assisted him in any way. The senior executive in charge of the meeting declared it closed. We walked back to the office. Hardly a word was said. Someone made a tea round and we carried on with our duties. We all knew something fundamental had happened, that something of consequence had taken place, but nobody knew what it was, or what the outcome would be.

I felt sorry for Mr Satchwell. He was a man who lived life according to the code of conduct he'd been initiated into, and the code was proving inflexible in the face of changing times. At its best it was robust, at its most unhelpful it was ridiculously inflexible. I'd never spoken with him: I was still a freelancer, and all business was conducted through my line manager, but it was like watching a man melting that day. He'd lost his capacity to define events in a public forum, and that's not what he deserved. He'd be gone within a very few months, but he was a good, principled journalist and an excellent leader.

There were afters to what happened that day, and the main one was that there was a mood to look inward for threats, whether it was the union – the NUJ, the National Union of Journalists – or senior staff, or individuals who were seen as troublemakers. Keith had asked the question. He was a maverick. All mavericks were trouble, and maybe the subs desk had had a part to play in it all too.

The whole drama was an example of how corporations can allow their gaze to shift from the external factors that were evolving in hugely significant ways, towards internal dynamics that were pretty much irrelevant in the wider scheme of things. When you get granular about it, business is soap opera: if you get lucky your firm's script will read like a Shakespeare play, if you don't have luck on your side it'll read like a Stephen King.

– Chapter 9 –

After 18 months as a freelancer at the *News* the financial situation was a mess. I was still claiming a government benefit for those on a low income, and the council house rent was being partly paid for by the state. But how much was subject to variations. What I really wanted to do was get a mortgage on the property, which was an option under the new Labour government's 'Right to Buy' scheme. But to get a mortgage I had to have a regular income.

I was regularly working regular five-day weeks for the *Cambridge Evening News* as a sub-editor and I had, by this point, a reasonable degree of competence, or at least I hadn't actually screwed anything up. I'd mastered the archaic technology, and had made no enemies, at least none that I knew of. I'd even done something quite unusual for a sub-editor: I'd written for the paper. Sure, it was just a "Last Night's TV" review, a column of about 400 words, but it was fun to do and I was asked to do a TV review every few weeks.

This was fine and progress was happening but it was proceeding at a snail's pace and I needed to come up with a plan to make the jump from a basic and insecure situation to something consistent. I talked to Mark about it, and he said I should ask about a permanent position. He suggested I raise the subject with Nigel Brookes, which I did at the earliest opportunity. This happened to be during a mid-afternoon lull in the newsroom, when the day's editions were all printed and the focus switched to getting ready for the following day's edition. Nigel was proof-reading some pages when I went up to him.

"Nigel," I said, "I've been meaning to ask you – I've been here 18 months now, and I'm enjoying my role, but it's getting quite difficult for me to have any sort of structure to my employment and I'm just wondering if there will be any full-time work for me here at any point?"

Nigel seemed ready for the question. "Well," he said, "there's nothing on the news desk at the moment, but there is a vacancy for a full-time role on the commercial features desk, and that includes the motoring section as well."

Commercial features is advertorial, where you write about how great a company is and they pay you for what is published. It's unequivocal praise and as such has a sign on it saying "Commercial Feature" or "Advertisement feature", like a health warning. But it was a full-time job, and the motoring angle was interesting. I knew a bit about mechanics, and I'd always had a good eye for a used car, so maybe that could be a good starting point. Slim, but slim pickings was all there was to go on.

"OK," I said, "so how do I apply?"

"If you're interested I can let you have an application form."

"Thanks – I am interested."

"OK, I'll bring them over to your desk later."

There was no formal interview process but a CV was required. I prettied it up a bit but needn't have bothered: I was the only applicant. Commercial features was considered a poisoned chalice, but to me it was an opportunity, and there hadn't had been too many of those for a while. The starting salary was £17,500 a year, pretty good given that the starting salary for a reporter was around £15,000. It felt like maybe I'd be able to provide my children with the means to make progress, to go to university, and have holidays – all inconceivable had we stayed in Somerset. Maybe we could buy a half-decent car.

So began the long and very unlikely haul to motoring editor.

– Chapter 10 –

Becoming the commercial features sub meant I had to move from the subs desk right across the newsroom to the commercial features desk, which was on the same table as the business desk in the corner near the editor's office.

It was difficult saying cheerio to the crew on the subs desk so I didn't bother but when you're a sub, the nature of the work means you don't go out. You're at your desk, all day, every day. You don't have meetings. You're considered a lightweight if you have lunch, unless it involves going to the pub for a couple of pints of beer, which some did on a regular basis. Sometimes I'd go along, just to be social, but I couldn't motivate myself in the afternoons following the lunchtime sessions so I tended to stay at my desk and maybe walk to the supermarket across the road to buy a sandwich.

The long hours of staying put meant you got to know your co-workers pretty well. You started to appreciate who was a morning person, who snapped under pressure, who would be the next one to make tea, and when someone would take a cigarette break. You'd find out about their likes and dislikes, what they watched on TV, which football club they supported. That was the norm, but with some, you'd get nothing. You had to take it or leave it, whatever. I tried to be friendly while making it clear that I'd rather have my toenails pulled out than be ingratiating.

Most likely if you work five days a week someplace you spend more awake time with your work colleagues than you do with your partner. It's like a marriage, or a commune: you try to avoid rows and hope to retain some sense of privacy or even mystery, if at all possible. Years later, when the business and commercial features desk was adjacent to an all-female features desk, one of the female writers told me that all the women on the features desk had synchronised periods for a couple of years. That was how close it got. That was how institutionalised you could get, sitting in a room with a bunch of other people for 40 hours a week.

Over on the commercial features desk there was one full-time commercial features writer, Ann Hubbard, and Lisa Millard, who was part-time, and I was the production guy. By this time – 1998 – we had ditched the old green screens and had PCs with Quark XPress, which I was familiar with from the days at Future, so I was on much more solid ground. Ann and Lisa sent me their copy and pictures and I put them on the page, made the copy fit the space, put a headline on, added the picture and a picture caption, and proofed it out for them to have a look at. If there were corrections I'd do them, before sending the page to the printer – by this stage all the typesetters and cut-and-paste merchants were long gone, and there was pretty much no one between me and the printing press.

Also on the desk were the business editor Caroline Swift, who was Mark's wife (though I'd never seen her when I visited his home), and Glyn Tucker, the business sub-editor. Glyn was old-school – a big bloke in his fifties, seen it all. One time he'd been deputy editor but it was rumoured he'd had some sort of personal worries and took the less stressful position of business sub. I knew from the start I'd have my work cut out to get him to accept me. To him, I was some flash Harry, some chancer who'd breezed in and would breeze out again just as soon as something better came along, and the sooner the better.

Like I say, it's important to be a good judge of character, but when someone gets me wrong and pegs me for something I'm not, I'll go the extra mile to prove otherwise. At the same time I could no longer afford to engage in battles I had no chance of winning. Such battles are massively time-consuming and arid, and only to be engaged in if unavoidable – like sitting on the same block of desks in a newspaper office. Glyn seemed like a bull who'd been speared one too many times already, and it was all about playing for time and staying away from the flashes of rage which still had the capacity to hurt. If I could avoid being gored, maybe I would have an outside chance of bettering my position somehow.

However, intuition indicated Glyn would find me irritating and furthermore that he saw himself as head-of-desk. If he got irritated, he wouldn't be able to have a go at Caroline because she was his boss, but me? Obvious target. In fact you might say that having a whippersnapper such as myself around was the last straw. He'd be keen to make sure I didn't get any fancy ideas above my station. No ideas was probably best from his point of view. I'd probably have to have balls of steel to outwit him, but I knew I couldn't duck the fight if I wanted to achieve anything at the *Cambridge Evening News*. I weighed up the odds: I was in my 30s and relatively fresh, I could probably last a year or two. That there would be a reckoning was clear: I tried to work out what form it might take so that I could be better prepared, but really I was only guessing.

Caroline Swift seemed constantly on the verge of imploding at this time. She was doing shifts in London for a daily paper as well as working at the *News*, and it was clearly a struggle to stay on top of her workload. And, because some of her workload was her husband, she was failing. I never really got to know her, I just wanted to stay out of her way and be invisible to her. No particular reason, she seemed nice enough, but she looked as if she was caught up in some vortex and I'd been sucked into enough vortexes to be wary of going near another one. I felt sorry for her too, and it's not good to feel pity for people, not in the workplace anyway: it weakens your ability to survive.

Ann and Lisa were great. Ann was Scottish, and talked plain English in a thick brogue. To her, the newsroom was full of men playing power games and she wanted none of it. She called everyone out on their bullshit. I liked her a lot. Lisa was amazing, she was so classy even talking to her I felt slightly geeky, like a clumsy teenager with bad dress sense or acne. Altogether it was a good team.

On the motoring front the stories were sent in by a local freelancer, Rodney Tibbs, who'd done all sorts of jobs for the paper – reporter, features editor, film critic – when he was working full-time. Rodney had started at the *News* as a tea boy in the 1940s, he'd seen it all and knew the chairman, Lord Iliffe, pretty well. Lord Iliffe, by all accounts, was one of the good guys. As someone who had followed the progress of Harold Evans' fate at the hands of Rupert Murdoch, I knew that publishers could be absolute bastards, but Lord Iliffe wasn't of that ilk, it seemed, and the *Cambridge Evening News* had an enviable reputation as one of the UK's most successful regional newspapers. The "man and boy" ethos was alive and well in this Iliffe newsroom, and Rodney Tibbs was living proof of it.

Rodney had retired from the office before I joined, and worked from home, but he'd been testing cars since the 1950s and kept his hand in, working as a part-timer from home. He was quite a legend, was our Rodney, and not just in the newsroom, he was well respected in the motoring trade as one of the best road testers in the land. Even in his seventies, he showed no sign of slowing down, but then again, being a road tester was one of the great jobs in journalism because when the motor trade launched a new car they would fly you off to Cape Town or Rio de Janeiro or Rome for a few days, and sweeten you up with food and drink and outings at these glamorous locations, so you'd write a nice report and send back pretty pictures for readers to swoon over. Who could not drag themselves out of bed in the morning when such exquisite delights awaited them?

I could understand why the *News* had mixed in motoring with commercial features, but it was clearly a mistake which would cap the potential of the supplement. They were two different parts of the trade. The copy for the motoring supplement wasn't pre-approved by outsiders: the motor trade didn't pay Rodney to write nice things, they didn't pay him anything, they just made it difficult for him not to write nice things. It was a supplement with commercial potential rather than a commercial supplement, and deserved to be carefully managed. The way I saw it, the motoring section was straight-up journalism, or should be straight-up journalism. Rodney wasn't answerable to the trade, he was answerable to readers, and he had to keep them on-side. If readers decided he had no integrity, that he was in the pocket of the car firms, they would dismiss his copy as puff, which would have meant he was finished as a voice, and he had enough self-respect to want to avoid that.

The end result was that Rodney would always be fair, and that meant pointing out some issues with a new model as well as the positives – maybe it was too pricey, or too slow, of there wasn't much room for passengers in the back seats. Whatever it was, he would include it: he was a journalist and as such he was impervious to the prospect of threats from advertisers. If they didn't like what he'd written, they'd say so, but his editor would always back him, unless he libelled someone, and if he libelled someone, that would be my fault anyway, for allowing it to appear in print, rather than Rodney's fault for writing it.

Pretty soon after I took on this new role we got email, which meant Rodney could send me his copy and pictures electronically. I liked that, it meant I could organise the supplement myself, without having to refer to or rely on anyone else. Rodney and I got on just fine. He knew I wouldn't cause him any trouble and maybe he suspected that I would bring something to the party, something which had been lacking until then: conspicuous success.

After a few months the faces started changing. Caroline left to live and work in London and a new business editor called Phil came in. He lasted a few months and then it was someone called Jenny Chapman, who was coming back into journalism after taking time out to be a mum and then a PR person. PR was public relations, it meant you earned a lot more money than a journalist, but you had no voice of your own. Jenny was hugely charming and had loads of smarts, wasn't obviously nosey, and was a very good listener. She seemed to have been biding her time in PR, waiting for an opportunity to return to journalism, and when she got the business editor's job she was polite but firm. I sat opposite her, I didn't have much to say to her and certainly our working lives never crossed. I was more concerned about Glyn, who appeared sour about the way the newsroom was evolving and seemed to want the clock to stop as soon as possible, preferably yesterday. I suspected Glyn was making Jenny's life difficult but she wasn't giving anything away on that front, at least while she settled in.

When Ann left for a PR role there was a gap. The job description in the advertisement for the role suggested that the commercial features and motoring roles were intertwined, but even though the motoring side of things wasn't necessarily a natural bedfellow with the commercial features side, it seemed obvious to get in someone who knew about motoring on the team who could also write commercial features, rather than a commercial features writer who would most probably know nothing about the motoring side of the job. It was apparent that the motoring section – a four or eight-page weekly supplement – could be jollied up a bit, but I couldn't do it alone, because I knew very little about cars. I didn't have sufficient knowledge to feel confident writing for the motors supplement, but I kept George Orwell's diktat in mind, that a writer ought to be able to address any topic and be able to find something interesting to say about it.

George Orwell is the master journalist, along with Harold Evans, and he understood the words trade like no one else. Here are his six tenets, each of which is encoded in the sub-editors DNA, or should be:

1. Never use a metaphor, simile, or other figure of speech which you are used to seeing in print
2. Never use a long word where a short one will do
3. If it is possible to cut a word out, always cut it out.
4. Never use the passive where you can use the active
5. Never use a foreign phrase, a scientific word, or a jargon word if you can think of an everyday English equivalent.
6. Break any of these rules sooner than say anything outright barbarous.

It was around this time I met Mark's son, Adam Swift, and lo and behold, Adam was a budding motoring writer, and he asked me if I could help him join the *News* just at the exact time the vacancy came up. It seemed obvious, it wasn't even a question I needed to stop and think about, it was just "how can I help engineer this?". The icing on the cake was that it would be a way to pay Mark back for all the effort he'd made to help me in the early days, when I'd been a total novice and way out of my depth.

After not much consideration I pointed up the application route to Adam, he had an interview and was appointed commercial features and motoring writer. But the big battles were always fought inside the newsroom, and I actually had no idea how Adam would cope when he found out what he'd let himself in for at the *Cambridge Evening News*. The workplace was like a social experiment as much as anything else – how long before your enthusiasm confronts the seemingly intractable mantra of: "This is how we've always done things round here"? And when that happened, history said there would only be one winner. But history was the story of the past, and new stories were coming along. Maybe the narrative would change, and if it did, maybe it would be for the better? I knew from the start that I'd have to stay the course to find out: once you've been in last chance saloon you know that the next card that's put on the table could be the last you'll ever see and you'll inevitably have to pick it up and turn it over to find out what it was. The alternative is just to put your life on hold forever, and that's no fun.

– Chapter 11 –

The situation on the desk, with Glyn attempting to have some sort of sway over how the team developed, ratcheted up incrementally.

I noticed an undercurrent developing between Glyn and Jenny, which seemed to involve him antagonising her. Whether deliberately or not wasn't clear, but that he was from a generation unused to taking orders from women probably didn't help. Maybe he thought Jenny was like Caroline, who would occasionally burst into tears when it all got too much. If so, he made a big mistake, and his misjudgement of Jenny's character played very well for me. Jenny was clearly a class act and that suspicion was confirmed when she was called into Peter Wells' office one day. As soon as practical I asked what it was all about. Apparently he'd told her that she couldn't claim mileage when driving her own car on work business. If she wanted to drive to a job she'd have to use one of the company's pool of cars. The pool cars were Minis, not the new BMW ones, the original ones made iconic in *The Italian Job*, the famous 1960s film with Michael Caine in it. The original Mini was basically a go-kart with a body on it. They were fun and dangerous. There was no way Jenny would drive one.

"Well, you've got to," Peter Wells had said.

"Well I'm not going to," Jenny had replied.

"You've got to."

"I'm not going to."

"Well you've got to."

"I'm not going to."

Apparently after a lot of this, the deputy editor, exasperated, said: "Well, what are you going to do then?"

"I'm going to consider my position."

And that was that, nothing more was ever heard of it, she got to drive her own car and the company paid for the mileage. I wasn't surprised: Peter could become a bit priggish when irritated. When riled, Jenny's frostiness could be felt in the Arctic, but you had to be really dumb to get on the wrong side of her. One time she had a spat with Glyn, who tried to get her to toe his line. When he went to the men's room she tutted about his behaviour. Her response seemed fair enough to me but I didn't want to get involved, because to get involved would have meant becoming collateral damage in someone else's drama. I needed to keep my powder dry, and Jenny would clearly be a formidable opponent, but she would never be my opponent, and it was obvious to me at least that Glyn had no chance in the wider scheme of things.

Meanwhile the motoring project was starting to get into gear. Adam turned out to be a fantastic motoring writer – witty, knowledgeable, with a love of cars. He started off doing the motoring news and left the road tests to Rodney. Rodney was too big a beast in the jungle to mess around with, but there was scope to develop the news side of the equation by adding features about safety or custom options into the motoring supplement, so Adam did some interviews with local car firms and the services they offered.

One time we set up a project which involved taking two 4x4s out on test and having a runout at WildTracks, a local off-road adventure site. That was fun: Adam did the write-up but I had to apply to my line manager, who at that point was the deputy editor, to get permission to take a car out for a road test. The off-roader, a Mitsubishi 4x4, wasn't booked via the marque's UK press office: Rodney dealt with that side of things, and he would – rightly – have been furious. The off-roader came from a local dealership who were keen for us to take the car out and write about it: they hoped for a mention of course, but without making too big a deal about it, so we had just enough leeway about whether to give them a plug to retain our self-respect. The deputy editor was happy to give the WildTracks project a green light because he could see the revenue trail and, to him, the supplement was a commercial project which required advertisers. If a journalist brought in the money, so much the better for him.

Adam started testing more cars and it was obvious that he was a bright young thing and his style of writing was just what was needed. The motoring media had traditionally been given over to fuddy-duddies but in the late 1980s a clever young chap called Jeremy Clarkson had single-handedly changed the whole schtick. Clarkson was a brilliant journalist, rather like Greg Ingham had been in the early days of the computer games industry. Clarkson was the first writer to draw non-motoring readers into the motoring section. He was like a stand-up heckler in print – witty, irascible, totally off-piste and wildly entertaining. By the mid-1990s he'd moved from print to TV, where he was the star of BBC's *Top Gear*, but he still continued his print adventure, which was a huge boost to all aspiring motoring writers. Suddenly it was cool to write about cars and be funny, and Adam was surfing that wave with great aplomb.

From being a sidekick, Adam became the star of the show and I was hanging on to his coat tails as the number of pages assigned to the *Cambridge Evening News*' motoring supplement went from eight to 12 to 16 and even to 20 pages. At its peak it would be 28 or 32 pages. The advertising team, led by a shrewd old-timer from Nottingham called Errol Bilton, spotted the opportunity and created new mini-supplements for special occasions such as the Formula 1 race at nearby Silverstone, and the annual registration plate change for new cars, which was a huge sales peak: advertisers flocked to the supplement when they realised there was a healthy and wealthy market in Cambridge.

The car trade in any case was on a roll: when the UK's motoring hierarchy realised that the new plate change was a great selling point – because people's vanity was stoked by having a new car with a new plate to show off to their workmates, neighbours and chums – they introduced a new plate change, so there was one in March as well as one in September. Everyone loved the boost to the trade: an era of excessive consumption had been triggered by relaxing financial regulations during the 1980s, and markets for houses, cars and holidays were coining new currency as the economy lost the steady financial mores of a previous era. The fact that much of the spending spree was financed by credit cards and complicated new finance packages seemed unimportant. No one knew where it was heading, and for a while it looked like win-win. For me and Adam that meant bouncing from the crest of one wave to the next with a sure-footedness that must have astonished our handlers. At its peak the motoring supplement was drawing in around £1.2

million a year in advertising revenue – an increase of something like 600 per cent from when we took it over. None of that meant diddly squat to my workmates, of course. They were all watching for signs of ineptitude or, worse, big-headedness, but we were too busy for any of that.

The inevitable showdown with Glyn came about when I took out a car on my own for a "first drive", which is an early preview – not a full road test, Rodney would do that, but a brief sketch. The local Audi dealership had approached me to take their new showroom demonstrator on. I checked it with out with Rodney and he seemed fine with it: by that point there were too many new cars coming on to the market for one person to cover anyway. It didn't affect Rodney's contribution because we ran both his road test and my first drive in that week's edition. There was plenty of space to fill and it was better to have in-house contributions rather than generic copy from the Press Association, whose services we were by then wired in to receive. Adam had been doing first drives for a few months already, but for me to do one was a definite statement of intent, and I knew there would be feedback.

Traditionally in print the motoring supplement comes out on a Friday. The idea was that people would buy the paper for the Drive supplement so they knew what cars to check out when they went to the dealerships over the weekend. Come the Friday morning when my first drive appeared in print, I got in as usual and settled down at my desk. Everyone was in: Jenny, Glyn, Adam, myself, and the wonderfully zany Philippa Danks, who had replaced Lisa and was by then writing most of the commercial features. After an hour or so

Glyn stood up, holding a copy of the supplement up turned to my review page.

"What's this?" he said accusingly.

"What's what?" I replied.

"This," said Glyn pointing at my byline. "You've put yourself into print."

"So it would seem."

"Well?"

"Well what?"

"Well have you passed your NCTJ training?"

The NCTJ – the National Council for the Training of Journalists – was the standard course for becoming a reporter. He'd punched right into my weak spot and he knew it. I'd had no training – I actually portray this as an advantage that allows me to write the way I wanted rather than the way I was "supposed" to, but the fact was that without that certification I could never be a reporter. Fine by me, I didn't much care for the way reporters' writing style was sand-blasted by training into a uniformity that verged on blandness. Anyway, that was my line. I found the whole culture oppressive, and wore my non-conformity as a badge of honour, but in fact it was a potential problem, and now here was Glyn trying to make my position untenable and there was nothing for it but go on the offensive.

"Okay," I said levelly, remaining seated. "I'll tell you what. If you've got a problem with my writing for the motoring supplement why don't you just take the issue to the editor, because he's the only person who can tell me to stop writing, not you. His office is right there." I pointed. "It's that door there." Of course he knew where the door was, it was just a ruse to deflect his rage.

"Well, did you have permission to do this?"

"Of course – just ask Peter."

Glyn looked at me, trying to work out whether I was lying. I stared back, then turned back to my screen and got on with my job, working in total silence for a good half hour. That was it in a nutshell: permission. In the old world, you had to have permission to do anything, but I'd come from a fast-moving new industry forged in the white heat of technology and there, it wasn't permission that mattered, it was all about whether it worked. If you did something dumb but it worked, you'd get resources. If you screwed up then the consequences wouldn't necessarily be terminal, because the whole idea was to try out new things and you got credit for trying.

The new rules were negotiable, there was flexibility. They were probably scary, these new rules, to the old guard, but the thing to remember was that it wasn't us who made the rules up: it was just how the economy worked. If you could read the runes, then good for you. The old surface had been tilted and there were winners and losers, but the new surface meant new dynamics, and I'd had my share of losing, which is why I'd gone to the trouble of asking my line manager for the go-ahead. I hadn't actually even asked him, I'd told him what I was doing, he'd had an opportunity to say no, and he hadn't taken that opportunity. That was all I needed, so I didn't need to worry about Glyn.

The showdown ended. He sat down, harrumphing somewhat. Nothing more was said. There would be no more attempts to block progress, and from then on me and Adam would sink or swim by getting results. At least, that was the theory.

– Chapter 12 –

New Year's Eve of 1999 I went to the fireworks on Midsummer Common. For about 20 minutes a spectacular visual display was splattered against the sky and I stood there with Jo and Em and Charlie, transfixed. Flo was out with her friends that evening – it being her birthday on New Year's Day there would be time for family later. My first experiences in the 21st century involved witnessing a colourful extravaganza with a long walk back to the car and a traffic jam on the Newmarket Road on the way home. Was this a metaphor? Maybe that'd be an overstatement, but there was an initial sense of hope that the new century brought with it a clean slate, then it was back to familiar sagas.

The 20th century had concluded relatively peacefully. Communism collapsed: the Cold War was deemed to be over in 1989 when the Berlin Wall came down. A new sense of peace in Europe meant nations could start planning for the future together via the fast-expanding European Union, which the UK had joined in 1973. Being in the European bloc was going okay but we'd got our fingers burned in 1993 when Britain's currency, sterling, had dropped out of the European Exchange Mechanism. It seemed that being part of a EU-wide currency bloc would be a step too far for us. But the country was doing well enough to ditch the fading Conservative party for New Labour under Tony Blair in 1997, and the mood music was that Britain had a lot to offer the world, and having a global financial centre in London did no harm at all.

But there were stirrings of chaos too. By 2000 the first wave of internet development had hit trouble. Firms which had nothing but a prospectus for an online business had been getting funded to the tune of millions of pounds before their site was even up and running. The City didn't understand the new technology, but it saw big profits and invested vast amounts. Then the dotcom bubble burst. A great many valuations and sales predictions were vastly overestimated. Too many companies which had been the beneficiary of huge investment in the last few years of the 1990s continued to post pitiful profits and many went out of business. Who now remembers boo.com, pets.com or Kozmo? Even Future Publishing wasn't immune. Chris had sold the firm to Pearson for £52.7 million in 1994 and then bought it back in 1998 for £142 million in a deal with Greg and Apex Venture Partners, but the magazines weren't selling any more. "I was losing $1 million a day, every day, for 18 months," Chris was to say in an interview with the *Daily Telegraph* in 2016.

The mentality that had allowed this to happen was akin to many other bubbles in history, starting with the great Tulip mania in the Netherlands in 1637, when the price of one tulip bulb cost as much as a canal house in Amsterdam. This was the first example of a futures market – a market based around what something would be worth in x years time. The point was, it was tulip *bulbs* which were the investment, not the tulips themselves. The tulips had a short shelf life, but the bulbs represented future growth, literally and metaphorically. The promise of even more profit in the future was what drove the price of tulip bulbs up until suddenly it became apparent the whole edifice was ridiculous, the bubble burst and the market collapsed. There are winners and losers both when a bubble develops and when it collapses, starting with those tulips and apparent in the Dotcom bubble as well, which burst in 1999/2000 (and more recently in the financial crisis which would ruin a whole lot more people in 20007/8). Such is the progress of financial architecture. Not only do we not learn, the bubbles are getting closer together.

There were other financial meltdowns of course: the Wall Street crash, the Japanese asset price crash in the 1980s, the day the UK crashed out of the European Exchange Mechanism – but the one in 2000 was disappointing because the new technology was supposed to have been our salvation, and here it was messing us up already. The markets were guessing, but they knew something was up, it was just that no one fully understood the potential of the new computer world as it dawned. Everyone was exploring and as usual well-qualified analysts were guessing and, when they risked being found out, they turned to bluffing, and when their bluff was called there was a crash. None of their antics made the bubble bursting any easier or the fallout for ordinary people more equitable.

For a while after that it was back to basics and there it might have stayed had not a new generation emerged from Silicon Valley, offering free software like Google and MySpace and FriendsReunited, whose monetary value would be revealed further down the line. That's what capitalism's about – taking risks. Google's founders had no idea they would be developing autonomous cars and creating talking robots with 15 years. There was no revenue model when they started because there was no revenue – that came later. To the risk-takers go the rewards, with a bit of trickle-down economics bolted on to keep everyone else sweet. That was the theory, until the trickle-down dried up, and then the whole mechanism was brought into question. Back at the start of the digital era the websites that took off – like Google – took off fast enough to be able to stay ahead of the game thanks to some truly incredible footwork in Silicon Valley.

Back at the *News*, the process of adaptation continued at a snail's pace even as the business world was in the throes of rapid change. In 1935, a company's average life span was 90 years: today, it's 18. We now know that the first lesson of business in the 21st century is that if you're not a disruptor, you're going to be disrupted – you can't sit back and wait this one out. But back then no one knew that, and there was a lot of wishful thinking. You can't blame the publishers of print media for failing to second-guess the future, but some people sensed they had to stay on the move and repeatedly raised their game. Chris Anderson, for instance, finally ditched out in 2001 and took on the chairmanship of TED, with massive global success. Steve Jobs was dreaming up iTunes. Amazon, PayPal, Yahoo and Google were all up and running. Facebook and Twitter took over where MySpace and FriendsReunited left off.

We got internet capability at the *News* in 2001. There weren't too many websites but being able to search information on Google made an immediate difference. The new technology made some jobs easier. Where once researching a story involved going to the library and asking the librarian for the relevant clippings from previously printed articles, and waiting for a quarter of an hour or so while the librarians looked through the cuttings, now we could sit at our desks, type in a few words and more information than we could possibly need was available almost instantaneously. That saved lots of time but it also meant that, gradually, the role of the librarians was diminished. Technology was making some jobs easier, but others were becoming obsolete. Maybe it had been ever thus, but there was a sense that the process had picked up speed. Eventually it became an out-of-control-express train that no one was driving perhaps except some AI algorithm: in retrospect, we were naive. But we were the first generation to have computers as part of our working lives, so there was no precedent for what was transpiring. It really was the Wild West.

The last librarian at the *News* was Lorraine Took. She was fantastic at her job, and clearly loved both the social and cerebral aspects of her role. When she was on duty you knew you would get a premium service that would grace the library of any Cambridge college, and she was utterly adorable to boot – smart, funny and considerate. When she left part of the paper's soul went with her, and it would get more and more like that as time went on. We all knew what was happening but, for the moment, print sales were respectable and there was no reason to suspect that the world wide web would become the news-spawning monster it would turn into, nor that users of the new technology would get their news for free…

The last time I saw Lorraine she was working at Cambridge's most-loved garden centre, Scotsdales. She loved that job too, she said, especially being outside and working with nature. They were lucky to have her but she had one of the best minds in the firm and her leaving was our loss.

Under New Labour, who were elected in 1997, Britain was being shunted down the road to being a service economy, with demeaning consequences for lots of people except property owners and shareholders. Businesses with overheads and pensions and vans and other infrastructure were seen as old-fashioned. Even hard work would become suspect: with a computer you could make money, why dedicate your life to incremental growth when you could strike gold with the right idea? The internet was a good thing in so many ways of course, but human nature is hard-wired simple and internet fame introduced the idea of short cuts into the minds of its users. Instant fame and fortune is so much more appealing than the hard slog.

For journalists the opportunity to just copy and paste words from one site into your own story opened all sorts of doors, and some of those doors led to the travesties of phone hacking, job losses on a mass scale, fake news and 'alternative facts'.

– Chapter 13 –

After five years, the situation at the *News* became more stable. Adam and I chucked out an amazing supplement every week. My transfer across the newsroom had been a big, if unlikely, success. But the churn went on: Mark left to work on Saga, the Folkestone-based magazine produced by the firm which provided services for the over-50s based. Glyn retired. An old guard of photographers, news reporters, feature writers and advertising staff dispersed.

The new editor after Satchwell was an apparently mild man by the name of Colin Grant, who didn't like conspicuousness, he liked regularity and order. Perhaps there were concerns about the way the economy was changing, but there was no appetite for a change in the status quo at the firm. Quite the contrary, they probably wanted to nail things down because everyone knew more change was inevitable. The cloth was gradually being trimmed.

The annual wage rise, for instance, became habitually bogged down in negotiations. It didn't help that the NUJ, the National Union of Journalists, was ineffective, and meetings went from impassioned debate to talking shop, where people could basically have a moan. The representatives the union sent up from London to help us address the issues we faced were pretty dreadful – self-aggrandising men who appeared impatient and bored, with little knowledge or even interest in working conditions and procedures. All their suggestions were platitudes. In any case there were nowhere near enough NUJ members to stop the paper coming out even if the entire membership walked out. It had happened once before: Glyn had told me in the pub one time – he actually wasn't a bad sort, and I respected him more than I have probably let on – about how a decade ago all had the NUJ members gone on strike and management had bodged together a paper anyway, even taking photocopies of proofs over to the press to get a single daily edition out. After a few fruitless years of membership I left the NUJ. If I wanted someone to help me out of a dark corner they would not be on my list of people I would turn to.

At this point I was becoming increasingly concerned about my parents' wellbeing. Both were in their eighties. My father had dementia and my mother had tuberculosis – possibly from her days during the war when she spent winters in freezing 'Nissan' huts with corrugated iron roofs which turned the rooms into fridges. I was visiting them in London every weekend. My older sister was living at home with them and my younger sister and her family had moved from Greece to Walthamstow in east London, to be closer. Meanwhile Jo was living across town in Arbury. She'd put Aggie up for adoption when she was five, and would come over on Saturdays and Sundays to be with her other three kids. I'd started doing shifts in London after chatting with my school chum, Adrian Bridge, who had seen an advert for subs at the *News of the World*, the biggest-selling Sunday newspaper on the block.

Adrian was working at *The Independent* at the time: he'd done the traditional journalistic route, starting with a qualification and then joining the *Bracknell Times*, a small-town local paper in Berkshire. His break came at the *Indy*. He was posted to Berlin just before the Wall came down in 1989, and his stories were regularly on the front page and tremendously exciting they were too. But just ten years later, newspapers started losing interest in having overseas correspondents. Europe was settling down, and maybe there would be just one reporter in Asia and one in the US: a lot of information on world events came down the wires and could be rewritten in-house – a development that would have scandalised a previous generation of journalists. Adrian pretty soon joined the *Telegraph* where he became production editor for the hugely successful travel section.

The 'News of the Screws', as it was called, was owned by none other than Rupert Murdoch, who had been the subject of a great deal of criticism by my journalistic hero, Harold Evans. Murdoch had been a media mogul since the 1960s: his break into the big time arrived when he started Sky TV 1989, and he had gone on to be the biggest media magnate the world had ever seen. I tormented myself briefly about whether to make the call to work on one of his papers and came to the conclusion that it was okay to take his money rather than put money into his hands – I'd not bought the *Sun* or the *Times* for decades. My family needed the money: my delicate nose would have to put up and shut up – and I was curious to know what the mechanics of the biggest-selling Sunday newspaper in the world would be like. So I called the number Adrian gave me and was asked to come in for some training. This involved going to Wapping, the infamous site where the once all-powerful print unions had been comprehensively outwitted in 1986.

The unions had dominated business life in Britain in the 1960s and 1970s. The car unions were the most vociferous, but the print unions were right up there with them. They decided what could and couldn't happen in the print sector until Murdoch sacked 6,000 employees and transferred the newsrooms of his major titles – the *Times, Sunday Times, Sun* and *News of the World* – to Wapping in January 1986. Murdoch had contingency plans for each phase of the strike and knew that the rail service used to deliver his papers would be strikebound too, so he hired haulage companies to do the distribution. Not a single day's production was lost during the year-long dispute and the much-anticipated boycotting of Murdoch's papers by the readers didn't materialise either. Apparently people didn't care much about how their papers were produced, and anyway the memories of the 1970s – when union power cut off vital services including waste collection, burying the dead and electricity – were relatively fresh.

It was hubris that allowed the unions to think they could continue the working arrangements of previous generations. For instance, there was an arrangement whereby workers would be allowed to go home when they'd finished their work, without remaining at their post until the end of their shift. This was one example of what was known as "Spanish practices". Of course there were no "Spanish practices" in Spain – it was just the casual bigotry of a generation who didn't get to go to Spain as much as people do nowadays, or at least did pre-Brexit. Anyway workers were paid to do a full shift but there was an assumption that you could leave an hour or two early, once the paper had been sent to press. This was clearly an anachronism. There were things you could do after the paper had been produced – prepare for the next day's paper, for instance. It ended up that workers were then paid a supplementary rate to do the extra hours they were already being contracted to do – a "Spanish practice".

Murdoch emerged from the Wapping dispute much strengthened and the union movement as a whole in the UK was effectively a busted flush, in which state it has remained, certainly in the publishing world. Clearly having your business run by shop stewards was not a good idea, but at the same time without unions the working population could be subjected to all sorts of difficulties without any means of redress.

Whatever the rights and wrongs, the food at Wapping's canteen turned out to be extremely good and very reasonably priced, which put me in a positive frame of mind. For six weeks every Saturday afternoon I was trained on using News International's computer system, at a rate of £220 per day – equivalent to three days' work at the *News*. After the training a green screen was found for me in a corner of the newsroom, on the sports desk. On Saturday afternoons I waited while the football games were played – between 3pm and 4.45pm. At half-time there would be some early reports but the main action started at around 4.30pm and built into a crescendo of mayhem and deadline-meeting which went on until about 6.30pm.

There's a situation in newspaper production called a "heart-stopping moment", which is when a big story breaks just before deadline. I'd had a few of these at the *News*, the main one being when a helicopter carrying the famous man-of-the-people Matthew Harding, the owner of Chelsea Football Club, had crash-landed and reports were coming in 15 minutes before we went to press at 8.45 one morning. My job was to cut the story back to fit in the text box on the page it had been assigned to, and add a headline and a picture caption. You had just a very few minutes to do this, and then the moments of panic – when the task seemed unbelievably daunting, and the clock was ticking as you desperately hacked at the story, all the while trying to keep the flow and rhythm of the report – would kick in. You had to work through your panic and get the job done in time without mistakes. There was no margin for error.

After you'd finished and printed out the proof and given it to the senior sub to send, you could relax for a minute before the next edition went out half an hour later. I learned how to do this without any guidance, it was just what you learned from watching those around you. The first task was to read all the copy through before you started cutting it back. During the first reading you'd be looking for ways the text could be cut, perhaps an elongated turn of phrase here, an unnecessary adjective there, and then whole sentences or even paragraphs if you had to be merciless, but the piece had to read well whatever adjustments you made. There was no way you could tinker with the design, to make a picture smaller or somesuch. You'd prune the copy back until the overmatter was all gone.

Even as you're doing the pruning you're trying to find the memorable words which would serve as the basis for a headline. The headline was another tricky bit. It had to fit. You could be two or three letters shy of filling out the deck –

a row of words – but no more. It had to be factual and also contain some sort of image or sense of drama, if at all possible. The "art of the possible" was what you had to explore, and quickly. Preferably something with a human angle, an emotional context which summed up the situation. You wanted people to see it and think: "Oh, crikey, let's have a read."

You also filled out the picture caption: if you were lucky the information about who is standing where, etc, is in the credits accompanying the picture, but if it was a generic caption and you needed more information you'd have to ask the picture desk. That was always a hassle. In most departments you'd get a basic level of service, but the parameters widened when it came to photographic community and they weren't shy of saying they were too busy but they'd do it within the next hour. Or so. You'd have to work really hard to get them to take any notice of your requests. In my case this would take at least a decade but once you were there, you were in. You got premium service. Until then it was a bitch-fest you'd rather avoid, but say the caption details were there, all you had to do then was get the page printed and take the proof to a senior sub or the duty chief sub.

Seconds could become hours while you frantically tried to work through the checklist and you prayed that something would come to mind for the headline to save you from ignominy. I tended to fill in the headline box as soon as possible, using any sort of words. It was fatal to stare at a blank headline box and try to imagine or visualise the words. What you had to do was get stuck in, try something –

anything – and tinker about a bit, ideas would come, and more often than not you'd get the word order right. But you had to be ready to start over at once if the idea didn't work or didn't fit the box. You had to do all this in maybe ten or 12 minutes when there was a rush on. And after all that you still had to leave time for the senior sub or deputy chief sub-editor on the next link of the chain to read it before it went to press, and change your headline if it wasn't up to scratch.

At the *News of the World* (*NoW*) there was a continual panic on the sports desk on Saturday afternoons and through the evening until about 8 or 9. At its peak, for about 90 minutes, you'd not take a toilet break, nor engage in any discussion unless absolutely necessary, you'd need perfect mastery of the technology and be possessed of a highly sophisticated subbing brain – that's why they were paying you top dollar.

I was unseated by the headlines for the games I was tasked to sub-edit. These were the football games in the lower leagues – the big Premiership games were covered by the top writing and production teams. Games involving teams lower down the pecking order were further back in the paper and not so important: they was my starting point. So I'd have a four-deck headline with eight letters on each deck to play with. Say Leicester beat Aston Villa in a game with a late winner. The headline would be "Foxes in late thriller at Villa". That would split nicely into four decks, as in "Foxes/in late/thriller/at Villa". Nice bit of rhyme there, got a bit of bounce about it: problem being you need to know the nicknames for all the teams. I didn't know Leicester City football club's nickname was the Foxes, and "Leicester" wouldn't fit. There was no Google on my computer either – it was another one of those green-screen throwbacks for whatever reason, and I was slow and my headlines were unwieldy too many times, so the sub-editor I sent my stories to would be probably exasperated at having to rewrite my headline. Not that he'd ever say anything to you, that was the point: you weren't even worth speaking to. Fact is, I wasn't a happy bunny on the *News of the World*'s sports desk and was pretty okay when they stopped calling me to book shifts after a couple of months. Anyway, what it would have said about me if I became a Murdoch henchman?

But even as I floundered, the culture fascinated me. When the first edition was done, everyone went to the pub, drank two pints of beer, then went back to work for a couple of hours. It wasn't a culture I was ever going to fit into, but it was a tradition that went way back, and to be part of it even for a brief few weeks made me curiously proud. It was part of the newspaperman's etiquette to be able to knock back drinks and go back to work. I could do the first bit well enough, but the second bit I wasn't so great at.

Even less fun was the cadre of the *NoW*'s newsroom prowlers – the men in suits whose job it is to make sure that everyone else is doing their job. I never liked these people, and at the *NoW* they were particularly mafiosi in their demeanour. Five years later, the paper was unseated in the wake of the phone hacking scandal after it emerged the reporters were illegally accessing the mobile phone messages of thousands of public figures – and not-so-public figures, as was the case for the family of murdered schoolgirl Millie Dowler, whose family had had their phones hacked in 2002, a fact which emerged when the case was finally heard in court in 2011.

The *NoW* court case put in the public domain what seemed apparent even from a cursory examination of daily life at Wapping. There's been lots of studies which show that people reach the top in corporate life by trampling on other people: in fact having psychopathic traits will help you get to the top in business – one in five business leaders is a psychopath according to a 2016 report by a forensic psychologist – and in pressured environments like Wapping it doesn't pay to have too many scruples. The public must have known their stories were being acquired using dodgy methods, but in time-honoured fashion suppressed any troubled thoughts until the truth was unavoidable. The police probably knew all about what was going on, but during the Wapping dispute News International, the publisher of Murdoch's title, had forged close ties with the Metropolitan Police hierarchy. Eventually some of the henchmen were jailed, but the ringleaders escaped punishment. Everyone sensed that the illegal hacking of phones was approved by those at the top, but it couldn't be conclusively proven. In any case the *News of the World* was closed in 2011: the final edition sold 3.8 million copies, a million more than usual. There's money in calamity, and lots of money if you do it on a grand scale.

What I learned from working in the *NoW* newsroom was that the enforcers we had in Cambridge were gentlemen compared to the thugs prowling the desks at Wapping. Not *like* gentlemen. They *were* gentlemen. The worst you could say was that they were like that nice uncle who could bang on a bit after a couple of drinks. It was more Captain Mainwaring than Don Corleone in Cambridge, thank goodness.

After the *NoW* escapade Adrian heard of another job going, on the news desk at the *Independent on Sunday*, after he'd left to take on the travel role at the *Daily Telegraph*. This was far more promising: I'd loved the *Independent* from the time it was first published in 1986. By the early 1990s I was regularly reading it from my Glastonbury eyrie, and was delighted by writers such as Andreas Whittam Smith and Robert Fisk, who were setting out a whole new agenda for what could be achieved in a newspaper.

Adrian's heads-up worked well – what a chum, there's facets of friendship that are so priceless and humbling. The deputy chief sub booked me in for some shifts at the *Independent on Sunday*'s Canary Wharf premises. The editor at the time was Janet Street-Porter. In those days in the regional press, of course, women didn't hold positions of power. It wasn't until I was doing shifts at the *Independent on Sunday* that I worked under a female editor. Janet Street-Porter was a big personality and a media star and commentator in her own right. Her tours of the newsroom were legendary: she would show up in the early evening dressed for a cocktail party in a tight dress with no visible panty line, an innovation whose practicalities I found obscure, with the result that one time I caught myself staring at her as she breezed past: perhaps I was trying to work out whether she simply wasn't wearing underwear. She seemed incredibly classy until she opened her mouth and a torrent of swear words emerged in a strangulated "Estuary" accent which was wildly humorous, possibly unintentionally so. Her ability to make a decision on the spot was her strong point: she had a lot of fans, and I was one of them, knickers or no knickers.

But the *Independent* had shaky finances and the turnover of staff was high. One time, having a tea break in a windowless room on the 17th floor, I heard that the editor, Rosie Boycott, had quit the previous day. One of the reporters there was crying, the stress was too much. "Another one gone!" she kept saying. They'd had several editors in very few years, it was a roller-coaster. After Rosie, for a short while, the editor at the *Independent* was Andrew Marr. He had a short and unhappy stint. I was asked to take a proof to his desk one time, but as I walked towards his office I could see he had his head in his hands and looked like a man beat, so I walked on and dropped the proof back later when he wasn't there. Pretty soon he became political editor at the BBC, and TV has proved a medium to which he is well suited.

The offices on the 17th floor in the heart of the capital had quite a view. As the sun was setting of an evening you could look out over London and see what an incredible city it is: in the suburbs where I was raised, such a vista was impossible to imagine. Other generations of Londoners in previous times would have been astonished to see the city like this. "Samuel Pepys eat your heart out!" was what I thought when I looked out of that window at dusk.

For a while the view added to the sense of being part of something special: it was a vibrant young newspaper, and the design was supremely elegant. It was a pleasure to sub the copy that came my way, especially Will Self's columns and anything by the great Robert Fisk, though the word was that if you messed up his copy, even if you made one cut he didn't like, he would finish your career at the *Indy*. I have no idea if that's true, but it made no difference to me. Once you were in the zone, a report of the Sermon on the Mount could come your way and you'd approach it just the same way, so that meant looking at Fisk's copy and trying to work out the primary facts and observations, which had to stay, but maybe there was a digression which could be cut to make it fit. The threat of being sacked, if it really existed, was more to do with correcting any spelling or grammatical mistakes, of which there would invariably be none, so you had to be double-sure that if you made any changes they were free of spelling and grammatical errors. I mean, fair play to the bloke, he's going out there, reporting on life in the world's most troubled war zones, risking his life to bring the news to the populace, and if some idiot sub screws with his copy he's entitled to go ballistic.

You never got any trouble from Will Self, though: he was laid-back to an astonishing degree and his copy was always sparkling, a good word count so very little cutting needed, and not just free of errors but resplendent in its use of the English language. I silently thanked my parents for sending me to boarding school: English was my first language. How difficult it must have been for my father, whose first language was French, to adapt.

The money wasn't quite so good at the *Indy* as it was across town, but it was still very good indeed – £180 per shift instead of £220 in Wapping – and it was a great place to work: there were no enforcers and everyone was treated with respect. The "pyramid" model of power flowing from the bottom up to the editor was being eroded, and everyone was expected to manage their own workload and responsibilities without having to refer to a superior for anything less than an emergency.

I liked everything about the *Independent* plus its Sunday edition and toyed with the idea of asking for a full-time job, but I couldn't ask my family to move again and the travelling would have been too much. And maybe I had reservations about returning to London: after ten years in Somerset, I'd learned to love being close to the land, and our home on the edge of Cambridge was working quite well – close enough to the city centre to be able to cycle in in 15 minutes, and far enough out to be right next door to the countryside.

Eventually the shifts at the *Indy* just tailed off too. The truth was, my headlines were being changed too often at the next stage of production: I wasn't getting it right enough, often enough. One day I rang in to ask about my next shift, and the desk chief who usually called me back just didn't return my calls and I stopped phoning in.

– Chapter 14 –

My father died in 2002. In his 70s and 80s he had resumed his practice of the Jewish faith, which meant going to synagogue on the sabbath, and reading his Talmud. This was a relief: so far as I know no one had asked him to put aside his creed for his family, but times were different – better – in his later years and he met with other Jewish people living in the area and seemed reinvigorated. His funeral service at a synagogue and Jewish cemetery was a complete mystery to me, however, which pained me somewhat, but Judaism in a matriarchal religion and my mother's Christian faith was what my sisters and myself had grown up with.

A year later Jo, after years of being sectioned and subjected to oppressive medication regimes which completely dispirited her, interspersed with agonising bouts of manic behaviour which she'd come to dread, took her own life. Jo had made at least one serious attempt on her life a couple of years before, which resulted in her stomach being pumped but, when the disaster happened, I was almost entirely unprepared for it. It was a crushing, crushing blow.

Treatment for those suffering from bi-polar disorder at the turn of the century was still pretty much in its infancy, and you couldn't but be bewildered by the rapidly changing medications put on the market by the pharmaceutical industry. I'd lost track of what they were after lithium and stellazine, there were so many more, it was a pharmaceutical blizzard. One time Jo told me she hadn't had a dream for a year, her weight fluctuated wildly, and there were difficult side effects including severe restlessness. But it wasn't stellazine that killed her. I'm not entirely sure what made Jo end her life on that particular day, but the fact was that I'd met her as a vivacious young woman and she had ended her days in tragic circumstances. If there's blame, it must be aimed at me. For ten years, we were married and struggling, then we were divorced, and in many ways the second ten years were much better because we didn't have to stay close, we didn't have to live together on and off, and we became more attuned to each other as time went on – as happens with married couples. But life can be harsh for people with mental health issues: it's hard to get a job for starters, and no doubt Jo felt an increasing sense of despair as the world shut its doors on her. Then came the events of 9/11.

The world got ugly when the Twin Towers came down on September 11, 2001. The last few times I visited Jo's house in Arbury – the last occasion being the week before she died – I noticed a large newspaper photo stuck on a door, a centre-page spread, of the second plane flying into the Twin Towers. Why would a newspaper print that image, I wondered? It came close to both glorifying the event and inflicting endless horror on the viewer. It was like being stuck in The Scream forever.

The aftermath to 9/11 was devastating: baser instincts overruled wiser counsel and the world set sail on a course with no destination and no motive other than revenge. The way the world changed alarmed lots of people, and for anyone with wellbeing issues such changes are deeply troubling. To some extent, people with mental health problems rely on the world treating them charitably. When there is no charity in the world, no compassion, folks are in real trouble. With 9/11, the era of terrorism was upon us and people of a fragile mental constitution experienced it in ways that left them further anguished and ever more isolated. It didn't much help those of sounder mind either, of course. After 9/11 there was a sense that everyone knew it was going to get so much worse.

Jo took part in the London march in early in 2003 to pressure the New Labour government to avoid going to war against Iraq. Iraq was a soft target, with a barely-plausible "baddie" in Saddam Hussein, whose regime had nothing to do with the 9/11 attack on the Twin Towers. The protest march was part of a coordinated, worldwide day of action to try and stop the coming carnage, and a million people were in London that day, but their voices were bypassed. Your voice not being heard makes you feel invisible, irrelevant, which doesn't help if you're already feeling marginalised.

There was no note. I hadn't spotted any immediate warning signs. I had a sense that something was wrong, but I'd had that sense for years and muddled along with it. Even so, it was doubly confusing: however close you are or think you are to someone, you still don't know what they're actually thinking unless they talk to you and, if they choose not to share with you – or can't share with you for whatever reason – you're just a blind person lurching round a desert hoping for a few drops of rain. And even if they do share with you, do you – can you? – actually listen to the clues of what they really mean?

The social and cultural fabric of the world began ripping apart – or being ripped up if you prefer – on and after 9/11.

The subsequent wars in Afghanistan and Iraq confirmed that 9/11 would usher in a terrible new cycle, adding to – though not beginning – the mutilation of humanity's hopes for peaceful co-existence. In such circumstances the first port of call is to be there for your family, in our case a wee band of brother and sisters that had already been through so much and now had to go through something potentially far more destabilising: the loss of a parent at a tender age.

– Chapter 15 –

Not being inclined to hark back to the past too much has sometimes served me well, sometimes not so well, but to dismiss the logic of history is not a productive strategy when world-changing events occur. The only way I could put the post-9/11 situation into perspective was to trace the historical antecedents which led to the abject start the world made to the new century.

The journey happened to start with my father's background. His Italian father and French mother lived in Cairo and Alexandra. Their son, David, was born in 1921: Egypt had been occupied by the British in 1882, during the Anglo-Egyptian war, then there was a protectorate run from London from 1914 to 1922, then there was a period of semi-independence until 1952.

The run-in to full independence was given additional traction by the creation of the state of Israel in 1948. Arab discontent had existed in Egypt since the original British protectorate but Israel created a new set of issues. What had previously been Arab land was seized to create the new nation: before 1948, there were occupations, but occupations end. Israel was welcomed into the United Nations a year after it was created. The issue of what happened to those whose homes were left behind became an issue, a niggling and still unresolved wound in global politics which found an expression in Egypt. King Farouk lost the throne in 1952, and former army officer Gamal Abdel Nasser conjured up a form of Arab unity and became president in 1956.

The West has never quite understood Arab sensibilities, putting expediency – its addiction to oil – above all else. There was no ethical component when it came to doing business with Muslim nations: theocracies, tribal alliances, dictatorships, demagogues – it was all just business. Anything could be overlooked or factored in, and that's still the case today. The 9/11 hijackings were carried out by 19 men, of whom 17 were Saudis. Saudi Arabia launched a cruel and illegal proxy war with Iran in Yemen, yet in 2017 arms sales from the UK to the Saudi regime totalled £1.1 billion.

Obviously no Arab state can win a conventional war with the West, so when their sense of injustice and grievance became too great they took actions which no soldier had consciously taken since the Kamikaze pilots of the Japanese Imperial Air Force during the final months of the war in 1944/45. Suicide bombings cause huge casualties but also inflict terrible psychological damage – to decent Muslims as much as anyone else.

The post 9/11 era quickly became problematic for the media to report. Politicians decided they wanted the press to echo rather than report the specific narrative they had chosen. Any attempt to scrutinise strategy or goals was portrayed as hostile to the interests of the nation and coalition forces. It got harder for the press to subject political decision-making to proper scrutiny. It is far too easy to draw a line between spin in the noughties and alternative facts in the middle of the new century's second decade.

The invasion of Afghanistan felt like a terrible idea. The invasions of Iraq and Afghanistan were masterminded by strategists who chose to put good sense to one side. Though the words weren't actually uttered until many years later, the leaders of the free world were saying 'we've had enough of experts'. The experts – historians, political analysts, economists – were ditched and the result was absolute chaos.

I'd been through Afghanistan twice: firstly in the spring of 1977, and then again that winter. Both times I followed the hippy trail along the Old Silk Road. The Road had reopened in the 1960s thanks to an interest in Indian religion among Western youth, starting with George Harrison of the Beatles. Since 100BC the Road had been the trade route for silk and cotton to be carried from China to Europe, and it was open for business for hundreds of years until the fragmentation of the Mongol Empire in medieval times, but it was still there. The bit I went on involved buses through Turkey to Tehran, the capital of Iran, then Mashad in the east and across to Herat in the west of Afghanistan, down to Kandahar and then up to Kabul and over into Pakistan via the North West Frontier.

The markets in Herat and Kandahar were full of incredible colours, smells, and goods, populated by people of incredible generosity and humanity that surged through you like a current of lightning with every smile, gesture and touch. It was an astonishingly vibrant culture, but on the way home that winter, after several months in India, the vibes were very different: the cold was incredible. There was no strolling around in the sunshine. I'd sat next to a young Afghan from Kabul on the bus journey from Pakistan. He was mildly westernised and spoke okay English. When we got to the bus station he invited me to climb the city wall and when we got to the top we had a smoke. As I looked out over a huge plain outside Kabul, the flatlands outside the city wall were lit up by tremendous flashes which initially looked like some sort of electrical storm, or possibly fireworks. A burst of light lit up the sky and, a half-second later, the noise followed. Then, as the smoke cleared, I saw tanks, and it became apparent that the rounds were being fired from their guns: the barrels had smoke coming from them.

I turned to my companion. "What's going on? Who's that firing those guns?" I asked.

"Oh, don't worry," he said with a wave of his hand. "It's just the Russians. They play their games. Soon they will be gone."

He swept his hand from left to right but, for my money, his blasé gesture didn't match up to the facts because there were probably two dozen tanks on that plain and I reckoned they were using live ammunition. I wasn't surprised when the Russians officially invaded in 1979: it was clear they had been preparing for their intervention. But then so had the Afghanis.

Afghani culture involves an incredible generosity of spirit but if you try to cheat them, or mess with their civility, you just made a big mistake because no foreign invader ever won an imperial war in Afghanistan. There were three Anglo-Afghan wars between 1839 and 1919 and in the first, the British army endured one of its greatest disasters when tribal fighters killed 4,500 British and English soldiers, plus 2,000 camp followers. Would we cast aside the lessons our ancestors paid such a dear price for to convey to us through history?

When the Russians left in 1989 I breathed a huge sigh of relief, and was absolutely gobsmacked when the CIA then got involved with the Taliban – whose numbers included Osama bin Laden – to overthrow the Russian-backed Najibullah government. The new Islamic state of Afghanistan forged after the Peshawar Agreement then brokered a power-sharing arrangement which involved the Taliban.

Anyone who has been to Afghanistan learns to respect the culture. The easy way, or the hard way, that's another story, but I often think of those incredible markets, and the people on the buses who were just the best travelling companions you could wish for. I wonder what happened to them all, each and every one of them. I still wish I could find out, go back through time and tag them or upload their memory banks into the collective history of 'civilisation'. With their permission, of course.

Eighteen months after 9/11, in 2003, a Western coalition – basically the UK and the US – invaded Iraq, overturned the regime of Saddam Hussein, and left a huge vacuum of power from which would emerge strategies and groups which conspired to wreck the established world order. And these dark clouds had a knock-on effect which wasn't confined to people with pre-existing wellbeing issues. Lots of people felt something very wrong happening, and those people were being marginalised or having their voices extinguished or turned off one way or another. The media wasn't there for them. The media had been coshed. The established ways of holding politicians to account were poisoned by spin doctors, who suggested that questioning any of the events leading up to the invasions was effectively treason. It took years to work out that the leaders of the US and the UK had had a private meeting at which they'd agreed to embark on an illegal war against Saddam Hussein, which took place even though Iraq had nothing to do with jihad. Indeed, given another roll of the dice, Saddam could have proved a useful bulwark against the Islamist revival. But it was not to be.

With the invasions in the Middle East in 2003 it was if another generation was being sent to the abattoir to suffer in the carnage of war, like their fathers and their fathers before them. Was it naive to have thought that maybe wars on such a scale were a thing of the past? There was a vast damage in terms of deaths, busted economies and wrecked lives, but one of the main victims of the Iraq War was the truth. Was it mad to think that David Kelly, the UK government's leading weapons inspector, may have been murdered in 2003? It was then: now, it seems rather more plausible. Did we really believe that prisoners weren't horribly and sadistically tortured in secret camps on their way to Guantanamo Bay? And the dreadful term "collateral damage", which meant women and children. Why did journalists allow the sanitisation of war to take place on their watch? And those Twin Towers, there were reports that there were explosives attached to the structure which were detonated by operatives working clandestinely for the American government – was it really possible that the engineering of the buildings would have allowed them to collapse like two decks of cards? Who could tell what the truth was in a tsunami of misinformation and lies?

This was the start of the alternative facts era. The seeds were planted by Western administrations in the run-up to the 2003 Iraq War to ensure the media toed the governmental line: "spin doctors" – propagandists – such as Alistair

Campbell were given high-profile roles by then prime minister Tony Blair and his attack dog Jack Straw. Their job was to ensure that anyone questioning the wisdom of an unprovoked attack on Saddam Hussein's Iraq would be bullied and ridiculed, undermined and sneered at. And where the facts could be altered, new 'facts' could be superimposed into the gaps. If you 'spin' something enough, the new slant gains traction. If you continually undermine the notion that the world is round, one day you'll be able to say that the world is flat.

Today, journalists are accused of all sorts of crimes, which is one legacy of the spin era. In the early noughties journalists were systematically cowed and coerced by politicians, and then distrusted by their readers when they submitted to the business logic of their owners. There's quite a lot of ground to make up.

– Chapter 16 –

By this time I was grateful just to have a job. Any thoughts of building on the back of my success on the motoring desk were abandoned in favour of just muddling along. The wind had gone from my sails. I was becalmed but I was lucky: my workmates were good to me, and my family was there for me, especially my sisters.

Jo died on a Monday, and I was back at my desk on Thursday when John Meredith, the sub, came over at lunchtime and said: "Don't you think it's a bit early to come back with all you've been going through?" I was grateful to him for saying that. He was right of course, and I took some more time out. And Jenny also really got to me when she said, referring to Jo again: "I'm so sorry, you were rather fond of her weren't you." Talk about English understatement.

The company treated me well. Any cockiness I had was replaced by gratitude. Mentally, a shift occurred: from being an unstoppable force of business logic to being a care in the community project. Without having a job to focus on, life would have been far bleaker.

Nor did the bereavements did stop there. My much-loved mum passed away in 2004, and 18 months later my beloved auntie Marjorie, who was the family's matriarch and the last of the Bond family from my mother's generation. With her, the last of the wartime generation was gone.

There was a dynamic to my mum's family which was remarkable in its spiritual orientation. This was made clear during an oft-recounted incident in Burma during the Second World War. My uncle Gerald had signed up, age 17, in 1940.

He fibbed about his age to join the Army – he was very tall, which helped – and was sent to the front line in India, where he took part in the Burma Campaign (1942-45) to rid the country of the Japanese. He quickly became an officer, and as a lieutenant he led a patrol near Japanese-held territory which became surrounded by Japanese troops. The soldiers concealed themselves and were hidden for a few days, but there was no way out. They were trapped behind enemy lines. They discussed what to do. There was no chance of fighting their way out: suicide was the only escape. With rations running low, they considered this possibility.

One evening, Gerald had a vision of his mother, Eleanor. She was apparently wearing the nurse's uniform she'd worn while serving on the front during the First World War. She appeared through the trees, and Gerald heard her voice: "Follow me." He ordered his men into a file behind him and followed the apparition through the jungle and, eventually, out to their own lines. Not a single soul was lost. When they walked back into camp, their comrades gathered to clap them in, a very rare event. It had been assumed they were all dead. Brave man, Gerald, who was awarded the Military Cross for repeatedly storming a Japanese machine gun nest on top of a hill with his Sikh sergeant at his side. Going uphill, under fire, over open ground, they had taken that hill. Gerald always had a huge respect for the Sikhs, Gurkhas and Hindus he commanded, so much so that it's in my cultural DNA. Always will be too.

When my mum, the children's grandmother, passed away I was in Cambridge, but within two hours we were all at the family home. I went into the front room where my mother lay, having succumbed to tuberculosis, which she may have acquired during the war, when she'd been billeted in iron-roofed Nissan huts which were freezing in winter. After being by her side for maybe an hour, I went out to the garden. Looking up, I saw a shooting star. It had a bright tail. Never seen one in London before. Looked like a rocket blasting away from the earth, carrying my mum heavenwards.

Comradeship was the only consolation at this time. Jenny was by now a properly good friend and colleague, someone I'd learned to trust as well as like, and it was around this time that we started having a regular drink "to chew the fat" at a pub in the nearby village on Fridays after work, a through-thick-and-thin ritual that was to hatch and breathe life into many ideas and strategies over the years.

Through the lens of these losses, life with my colleagues took on a new aspect. Where there are people, there's stuff, and yes I now had this huge tragedy to try and make sense of, but when I looked around there was all sorts going on in the newsroom. As with any walk of life there were people with issues, alcohol issues, or in the throes of divorce or serious medical ailments, people who went off sick for months, people with hopeless relationships histories – all sorts. I went from someone on a fairly modest rung of the corporate ladder, pushing ahead with some success, to someone who was treading water, but along the way I learned a lot about the way the company treated its staff and, when you were in trouble, working for the Iliffes was really good. They looked after you. It was quietly impressive.

I was still working hard but actually I'd already reached my ceiling at the *News*. This wasn't computer games, this wasn't magazines, this was newspapers: there was no room for, or interest in, new ideas and no new challenges. The vertical growth I'd experienced as an entrepreneur was never going to happen in this environment. Challenges mean risks, and risks unsettle the bottom line, and holding the bottom line was now the whole of the story.

If I wanted to stay at the *News*, that was fine, but if I hoped to rise any further through the ranks, I was kidding myself. I wasn't really a newspaperman, I was still impersonating a newspaperman – doing it with some aplomb, but not in a way that made me promotion material, and suddenly I was glad of that. I could do my job pretty much like clockwork, but behind the professional competence which was by now second nature lay private grief, and behind that I was slowly failing, collapsing into a turmoil of self-doubt and grief. And there I would perhaps have stayed, becoming increasingly incapacitated by suffering, had not management made the mistake of picking on me. I don't know why, perhaps it's true what they say about smelling fear or weakness: in the business world being weak is not a strategy that brings too many dividends.

The process began when an advert in one of our weekly papers had abusive text inserted by a disgruntled employee. I had no idea who did it or why but the copy was changed to read something offensive towards the paper's management and it was on a page which I had access to. Being the commercial features and motoring editor gave me access to roam anywhere on the electronic system, so I could open pretty much any page the company produced and mess around with it had I been so inclined. That wasn't my style of course, but the editor thought otherwise and called me into his office.

"We had a problem with one of the ads on a page in the *Cambridge News & Crier*, Mike."

"Yes," I said, "so I heard."

"Was this a page you worked on?"

"No, it wasn't, Colin."

"Do you think this sort of behaviour is acceptable?"

"Not at all, of course not."

"And you're sure that it wasn't a page you worked on?"

"Very sure, there's no editorial work on the page that involved me."

"OK, but do you know who did it or might have done it?"

"No idea, Colin."

The next time, a few weeks later, he upped the stakes. There was an error in one of articles, a few stray glyphs which I must have put there while rereading the page just prior to sending it. It read something like "... this is a five-star@!∂ moped which is available from local firm Mopeds of Cambridge".

Colin called me in again. What was I trying to do by inserting this mishmash at this point, was I trying to insult the moped firm in some way?

"Colin, I work very fast," I told him. "I have dozens of pages to produce through the week and on this occasion I must have somehow put some sort of keystroke in the last read-through before sending the page to press and that was what appeared in print."

"What keystroke?"

"I've no idea, it's not something I've done before."

"Ok thanks, Mike, but I'm not satisfied and I'm going to send the page off with the computer trail to a London agency to find out who did this, and they'll come back with a complete history of that page. That way we'll find out if this was an accident or not. Do you understand?"

"Of course."

"Is there anything else you'd like to say?"

"No."

"OK thanks Mike."

I left. I was shaking. He was asking me to confess to something I hadn't done. Right at that moment, I thought he was the biggest jerk I'd ever met. In retrospect, of course, I should be thankful because it was the first time I'd felt any fire in my belly for many moons. Even if he didn't know it, Colin's behaviour kickstarted my survival instinct, and for that at least I'm grateful. Not to him, though. To Great Spirit.

Although neither situation was mentioned again, the implication irritated me. It felt like "they" were targeting me, and for a while I was very unsettled, and then I got stroppy. If I was going to be seen as a troublemaker anyway, maybe I should give them some ammunition. In any case, I had rights, and it was time to exercise them. In particular, the motoring supplement was getting so huge that there was a team of six advertising motors reps selling into it full-time, and their bookings started getting messed up, which meant I had to redesign pages close to deadline on a Thursday afternoon. Advert bookings were officially supposed to stop 24 hours before the print deadline but the motors manager – still Errol, joined by some hungry young sidekicks – couldn't resist trying to sneak in late adverts, and he was in the habit of getting his way. But that didn't mean the rule had been suspended, it just meant it was being overlooked, and I gave ample warning that this situation was temporary.

One Thursday afternoon when a late advert came in I told Errol he had missed the booking deadline and the page was done and ready to go. A couple of minutes after putting the phone down the deputy editor was at my desk.

"Mike, there's a new advert come in for one of the motoring pages. Are you aware of it?'

"Yes, but it's way past deadline."

"OK," she said, "but it needs to go in."

"That page is done, Debbie, maybe the ad could go into the classified section?"

"It needs to go on that page, Mike."

We stared across the divide a moment, then she said: "So are you saying that you'd prefer me to get someone else to redesign the page?"

"Well, that would be a great help, yes, thanks."

From that exchange, a disciplinary procedure for refusing to obey an instruction was brought against me. The process was deliberately glacial. A formal letter was delivered by hand to my desk which stated that I would be required to attend a disciplinary session later the following week. I had several days to stew on it. The key point of my defence was going to be that I hadn't refused the instruction, an alternative plan had been proposed which I had accepted. But still, it was Debbie's word against mine, and there would only be one winner.

The outcome of the disciplinary procedure was that I was put on a final warning, which would stay on my record for three years and then be scrubbed. Any further disciplinary issues in this period would result in instant dismissal. Not quite the revenge I was hoping for, perhaps, but the late bookings stopped pretty smartly anyway, and thereafter I never had any dialogue with the editor or his deputy if I could avoid it.

In any case a more important saga was brewing with Adam, who had fallen in love with another member of staff. Helen ran the firm's charity fundraising department on the other side of the newsroom. They were clearly smitten with each other but there were complications: a senior, and older, colleague also had the hots for Helen, plus she was married to a policeman in the Metropolitan Police – not someone Adam wanted to mess with or be messed by. It was an uneasy time but the way the cookie crumbled was highly unexpected.

In 2004 Colin was replaced as editor by a colourful character called Murray Morse. It seemed that the paper's circulation was falling rather too rapidly for the boardroom to ignore, and someone with new ideas was hired to turn sales around. Colin's style of management – like we were a branch of the civil service – hadn't generated results. In particular, he'd boxed himself into a corner when the features editor had left a couple of years previously, and he'd decided this was the right time to shut down the entire features department, so for two years the *News* didn't have a features team. This act of vengeance risked damaging the product. In terms of getting results, it cut the salaries of four or five people, including said editor, Angela Singer, the very able theatre and film reviewer

Alan Kersey, and David Etchells, who had been father of the chapel (the chief NUJ representative in the office) for many years, but it meant the paper had no features in it. It was a ruthless decision, made for reasons that didn't have much to do with producing a better paper. I wasn't sad to see Colin go.

Murray, the incoming editor, was an old school journalist – a former News International executive, no less, from the *Sun* – and a tough talker with a big thirst. He was one of those blokes whose vast belly seemed to be a source of pride, for reasons I've never fully appreciated. Whatever, it needed gargantuan appetites to sustain it and Murray was evidently up to the task.

Opinion is still divided on Murray's turn at the *Cambridge Evening News*, as it was still called when he arrived in 2004. Some say he was refreshingly brilliant at letting his staff get on with their job without interference. Others insist he was reckless and his enthusiasm for sensationalism was "not Cambridge". Indeed, at one point protestations by city burghers who were made it plain to the owners that the paper was "going in the wrong direction". But overall Murray's editorship was positive. Some of this was simply because he wasn't Colin, but it's also true to say that he wanted people to be creative about their work, and try new angles and ideas. He'd back away from the boring stories about transport matters (an obsession with traffic-bound Cambridge residents) where possible, and try to focus on issues such as the behaviour of the region's travellers, homelessness (a huge problem in the city), the incredible output of the local artistic community and the excesses of university life.

Murray attempted to be a forward-thinking editor on his mission to turn around the ailing fortunes of the *Cambridge Evening News* but, knowing he had thrived in the culture at Wapping, it seemed wise to steer clear of him as much as possible. By this time I just wanted to have as little contact with management as possible. As it turned out my main interactions with Murray occurred when I developed an eye problem and asked the company to get me a flat screen.

Over a period of several weeks, I'd noticed that after a few hours in front of a computer screen I was getting a stinging sensation in my eyes – and it was getting worse. At times it was as though the surface of the eyeball was being scratched with fine glass: blinking was agonising. Eventually I went to see my GP, who referred me to an optician for tests. The tests were inconclusive, but the optician suggested that I may have some sort of aversion to computer screens. I was informed of scientific reports on the effect of long-term use of computers which I tracked down and read with great interest.

In the early days of the computer revolution monitors were basically TVs. TV technology in those days meant cathode ray tube technology. Cathode ray technology basically means a gun firing electrons that make up the screen display. There are three electron guns – red, blue and green – at the back of a cathode ray tube, each producing a different stream of particles. Each stream travels to a metal plate with tiny holes punched in it, called a shadow mask. Travelling through this plate the three streams from the red, blue and green electron guns combine to form a pixel. The three streams are mixed into thousands of individual pixels which make up the screen display. The display that the user or viewer sees on the screen is the result of the discharge from the electron guns and some of this discharge is projected right out of the screen and impacts the air around it. This air is changed, it becomes charged, and this has an effect on the user or viewer. Usually this effect isn't noticeable, but for some people it is. They are affected by the electronic discharge because it messes with the liquid covering the human eyeball. This liquid has two components – oil and water. The oil comes down through the upper eyelid and is distributed on the surface of the eye. The liquid comes from the tear ducts, which stretch from the eye to the nose, and together the two liquids provide the delicate covering that helps make the human eye the remarkable and beautiful instrument it is.

There are two ways this balance of liquids can go wrong. One is if too much oil is produced, the other is if not enough water is produced. Either way, the outcome is a condition called dry-eye. Dry-eye is the condition I was almost certainly suffering from, was the conclusion of the Cambridge optometrist I saw after following my GP's advice. And the report made it clear that the condition could be exacerbated by computer use.

I did some more research – Google was up and running, and more scientific research was being made available on the internet. It was clear that the new type of flat screen technology could be a solution. The display on a flat screen involves a different technology composed of liquids. No electron gun is in use, so your eyes are not being bombarded with a tiny electric charge when you sit in front of the screen. It seemed pretty obvious: surely my employer would pay for a flat screen if it made my working life bearable. Indeed there were some flat screens already in use in the newsroom, allocated to the designers for the most part but also some others, including on the subs desk.

It seemed obvious, but there's a small proviso to that – it seemed obvious to me. That didn't necessarily mean I would get a flat screen. I mean, I bought a flat screen for use at home, but acquiring one for work purposes turned out to be a long and rather painful journey.

– Chapter 17 –

The findings of my research into flat screen technology were duly presented to my employers and they said they'd have a look at it. Nothing was heard back for two weeks, then I asked the editor's secretary, Vanessa Whitworth – another role, along with copy runner, off-stone sub, librarian and office manager, that would disappear within a couple of years – what the situation was. The very wonderful Vanessa, who became the managing director's secretary after her job was devolved away from the editor, was very helpful as always and said she'd get back to me, which she did a few days later: it was being looked into by the HR – Human Resources – department.

Normally the editorial and advertising departments wouldn't interact with the HR department and when we did it usually meant bad news. Put it this way, they didn't often ask you to pop by to offer news of your salary increase. HR was an elite corps, less approachable than the accounts department, and all-powerful – they could be the first and last people you'd see at a firm. It's hard to account for the way corporate HR departments have swelled in the last two decades, but I guess if you're put in charge of a firm's employment strategy, one of the strategies you might want to consider would be how to enshrine or at least maintain your own role within the corporate structure. Of course, they're usually very nice people when you get to know them, but there's always the residual knowledge that they have rights and powers that ordinary mortals can barely conceive of.

Time passed and the eye condition got worse. My anxiety level was rising to "very fretful". By early afternoon, four or five hours after starting my shift, it began to feel like someone was scratching their nails into my eyeballs and dragging their claws slowly downwards. It was excruciating agony just to continue sitting at my desk. I tried to get up as often as possible. I blinked a lot less than usual. I switched my eye away from the screen to look out of the windows at the trees in the nearby country park. One time I saw a young deer stray into the car park, and waited with baited breath until it finally found a hole through the wire fencing to escape through. Of rabbits, squirrels and foxes there were plenty. It seemed like the world was going on while I was trapped in a metal box being subjected to a rare form of torture.

I did more research and the science started to stack up. It was a straw to clutch on to, of course. What was the alternative – I was going blind, or I had something catastrophically wrong that would make it impossible for me to work in front of a computer screen again? I stopped watching TV at home. I implored my line manager to ask HR to take account of the research coming out. We were, after all, the first generation to be working for long periods of time in front of a computer. The consequences in terms of eyesight, musculature and wellbeing were unknown.

My line manager at this point had changed. Debbie had left for a role in an organisation in New Zealand, and the new line manager was a bright young executive called James Foster. In his first week, on the Friday, James called me in to his office.

"Sit down, Mike," he said, pointing at the chair opposite.

"Thanks James," I said.

"Now as you know I'm the new deputy editor and your line manager," he said, "and I want you to know I'm never going to bring a grievance procedure against you, Mike."

I was startled. I nodded. "OK," I said cautiously.

"If there's a problem, any sort of problem, then we need to talk about it – to work through it and sort it out. Is that okay with you?"

"Of course, thank you, that's really good to hear."

"OK, thanks Mike."

I didn't like hustling James for updates on my flat screen. It was a budgetary decision, one the editor had to make. James seemed broadly supportive of my position but he had no control over the payment.

Flat screens in 2004/5 were quite expensive, maybe £600 for a good one. The trajectory of the technology curve was already established. When a product became attractive enough, early adopters would buy it, even when it was expensive. When sales took off, prices came down. If consumers wanted something enough – if the technology had enough value, or perceived value – they would find a way to acquire it. And flat screens were elegant and cute, plus the display was better than the cathode ray equivalent. Flat screens took up much less space on a desk, and were far less hassle to move around. Many workforces had been using them for years. It was just a question of time.

Anxiety turned into stress, and stress is difficult to control. I didn't trust myself in the workplace any more. If nothing happened soon on the flat screen front, I would have to go off sick – it was either that or I would say something stupid and get myself fired. So one afternoon, at the end of my tether, eyes burning like hot coals, I simply got up and walked out.

The furore was two-fold. One was that I was off sick and the second was that I'd walked out without telling anyone. In corporate terms, this is the act of a prima donna, someone who has got to be brought into line quickly or let go of. But in human terms, I was under a lot of pressure. I had a problem with my eyesight. I presented a solution which was rejected on the grounds of cost but to me, my eyesight is priceless. My position was non-negotiable and the stonewalling had to be met head-on.

After the melee of emails and phone calls died down, I was signed off by my GP for stress. The GP gave me two weeks off and I had to go and see her again in two weeks' time. In my email correspondence with my employers at the *News* I made it clear that the stress I was experiencing in the workplace was related to my deteriorating eyesight, and the lack of progress in implementing the proposed remedy. At the end of the day I knew the reason for the prevarication: if I had a flat screen, everyone would want one, and that would be expensive. It was a delicate situation.

After two weeks off I went back to the GP and got another two-week sick note. I was prepared for this to go on for a very long time, however long it took, in fact. Midway through this second period I got a letter in the post from the head of HR, Graham Judge. The letter was for an appointment at the Spire Cambridge Lea, a private local hospital, to see their optometrist the following week. Would I agree to go? Would I!? I was delighted, it offered a formula to end an impasse with neither side losing face. All I had to do was trust that sense – and science – would prevail.

Chapter 18

Sense and science did prevail – eventually. I went for the test at the private hospital. It was very thorough. My condition was described as 'dry eye'. The treatment involved taking hypromellose eye drops as often as necessary, and being in the open as much as possible. If I had to work in an office I would need wrap-around prescription sunglasses which protected my eyes while using a cathode ray tube screen. I went back to my optician, an excellent professional and top specialist called David Murphy, and his team fitted me out with a set of orange wrap-around shades similar to the ones used on ski slopes. The shades allowed the user to clip in plastic lenses rather like those pince-nez the old boys had sitting on the bridge of their nose a century ago, and I could clip this pince-nez into the sunglasses for reading (I'm long-sighted) and unclip it when, for instance, I wanted to use the sunglasses while walking or cycling.

Mr Murphy explained, when he read the notes from the Spire, that I had an unusual form of dry-eye. The most common form occurs when the tear ducts are under-active and generate too little water for the eyeball: this wasn't my complaint. The tear-ducts were doing fine, but too much oil was being produced. The oil was produced by the Meibornian glands in the upper eyelid, and mine were misfiring, and too much oil was being squirted on to the eyeball for the tear ducts to produce a balanced liquid. The hypromellose drops would reestablish the balance. And indeed, the drops – basically slightly salted water – I still use a couple of times a day, and I'm very fortunate to be able to say that the condition, though it hasn't improved, hasn't worsened either.

The next step was to go back to work. All I had to do, I told myself, was not mention the flatscreen, even verbally, let alone in an email: any mention of the topic could have been construed as blackmail which would have resulted in instant dismissal. I didn't trust Murray or Graham Judge not to play that card: I had caused a lot of trouble.

It wasn't easy to walk into the newsroom and go back to my desk after several weeks, but life goes on and I picked up where I'd left off. I looked ridiculous in my orange wraparounds, but I was a living reproach to the bean counters, and I was happy enough. I still in the saddle. I was funding Em and Flo through university as best I could.

After a couple of weeks the editor called me in. It was a Friday morning, and Murray was in his office with James, who looked uncomfortable. He pointed to a chair beside a small, round wooden table. I sat down. He sat down. James was already sitting down. Murray went through some preambles – the stuff that had to be said, in corporate-speak, stuff like "the company has paid for a private assessment and has demonstrated its commitment to following Health and Safety regulations at all times". There was no way Murray was having any fun with this and when he'd finished he chucked the papers down on the table and glared at me.

"What's going on here, then, Mike. It's like you've got a vendetta against the company going on, what's it all about?"

"I'm just worried about my eyesight, Murray."

"So tell me this," he says, and he's a big man with a massive neck and it was bulging in ways that made it clear that I might have really pissed him off. "Tell me why does it feel to me that I've got the fucking sword of Damocles hanging over my head, what's that all about then huh?"

I've had a thousand icy, cutting remarks said to me directly or within earshot in my time, but the times when I've actually managed to satisfactorily land a killer blow back are very rare: fortunately this was one of them. I mentally prepared myself to not betray a single shed of emotion in what I said next. Whatever it might be – and I had no idea what words would come out of my mouth – I was going to say it very, very slowly and very, very calmly. Nor would I even do so much as blink.

"I think you'll find, Murray, that I'm the one with the sword of Damocles hanging over my head and my future employment prospects in this industry."

I looked him straight in the eye. The comment was a direct hit. Up until then I was just a procedural irritation to Murray but for me, my eyesight was endangered. The chasm was there for all to see. Once he understood that I was absolutely, in all seriousness, not going to back down in front of his machismo-fuelled comments, the bluster remained, but the fury was synthetic. A few more points to note going forward, and the meeting was over.

A couple of weeks after that, I arrived at my desk one morning and there was a new screen on my desk, installed by IT. A new, flat, screen, one that was big enough to design pages on, not just act as a word processor. The long, elliptical, tortured quest to resolve my eye condition was over, but it had gone on so long that I'd not noticed what was going on around me, and in particular what was going on with Adam.

Adam was happy to have found Helen, and things were working out well for them, but falling in love with a work colleague inevitably brings hurdles. Her role was to run the firm's charity arm. A charity arm at a newspaper might seem quaint today, but at the time we were seen as a community newspaper by the owners, and distributing some of the firm's largesse – and publicising the fund-raising activities which took place in the community – was a job in its own right. The Iliffes knew which side their bread was buttered and giving back was always part of the business model. However, it's difficult to focus on your job when you're in the middle of a love affair…

From Adam's point of view the situation was manageable, but slightly awkward. And then all the dynamics that seemed to keep the playing field stable tilted – or were tilted, depending on your point of view – all over again.

Murray had sent out an email stating that the wages model in the newsroom needed to be more consistent and that every reporter should be earning a minimum of £21,000 after five years: if anyone wasn't in that category then could they come forward and the anomaly would be rectified.

Shockingly, this included Adam. The wages structure in the regional newspaper industry is on the low side, but the situation in Adam's case had been absurd for some time, and here was a chance to have an income that reflected life in a city which was becoming increasingly expensive to live in.

All the paperwork for Adam's salary reset seemed to be going through smoothly and after a couple of weeks he was starting to become gratified about the way he was being treated. For a South African, maybe all Africans – maybe everybody – respect is important. In Africa they don't do business without first finding out about the person they're dealing with. Does he have family – brothers, sisters, sons, daughters? A man who has family is answerable to something bigger than money. Who are his acquaintances and friends? Can he dance? Only after a bond has been forged can business begin. The bond hadn't been fully forged for Adam at the *News* and now that prospect was within sight.

Then, an email from Murray. Could Adam go to his office and sign the paperwork? I wished him luck and off he went. Back at his desk a few minutes later, he said it had all gone through smoothly and Murray had forwarded the paperwork to HR to sign off. In any previous era this would have been a formality. But we didn't know how times had changed until this fateful afternoon.

Half an hour later, Adam was sitting at his desk when he was asked to go back in to see the editor. He went in puzzled and a minute later emerged furious, and stomped back to his desk. He started swearing – and South Africans don't hold back once they're in the mood. I'm sitting next to him, and I can see he's going bananas and also that he's going to send an email, almost certainly to Murray but possibly also to the HR department, the managing director, anyone and everyone – he was past caring.

We had this agreement, me and Adam, that we would act as each other's email alarm. The adventure and element of novelty that the internet had provided in its early days had already waned. Too many times things had been said in an email written in haste, when feelings ran high. It didn't help that when it came to recipients there was an "all" listing, which meant that your email would go to everyone in the whole company – everyone from Lord Iliffe down. There had already been a few mishaps. Pretty soon the "all" option would be deleted, but that hadn't happened at this point. In any case this was not a good time for Adam to send an email: later, he would cool down, but if he pressed 'send' someone else would be in receipt of his fury and that would invariably come back at him.

As Adam was typing this email I was praying he wouldn't send it without asking for a second opinion, but it got sent regardless and afterwards there was a sense that bridges had been burned, that oxygen had left the building. Later, he told me what had happened. HR had blocked his wage increase on a technicality: he hadn't passed his shorthand test when he took his journalistic qualifications and HR had said that because of this he couldn't be classified as a reporter and therefore wasn't eligible for a salary of £21,000 after five years' service. There was no way back. It mattered not one jot to HR that he'd been doing the job for all that time and there had never been a single complaint. I'm pretty sure the decision surprised even Murray, who discovered the hard way that the rules had changed and the HR cadre now had the power to overrule his decisions.

Adam's stint at the *News* was coming to an end. A few weeks later he'd found a new job working for *Auto Italia*, a motoring magazine for Italian car enthusiasts based 20 miles down the road towards London. On the day of a long-standing member of staff's departure it's custom, in the print industry, for the editor to make a speech about the departing staff member, and to give the leaver a front page with a witty resume of his or her time at the paper. Adam's speech was given by James Foster, and it was very funny. He referred to Adam's leaving as "breaking up the newsroom's Lennon and McCartney". You had to laugh. Who was Lennon and who was McCartney?

I was pretty numbed out, not just by the fact that Adam was leaving – I'd sat next to him pretty much every working day for seven years, he'd proved to be a properly durable brother in arms – but also the manner of his departure, the lack of grace shown towards someone who had been a good employee, who'd worked hard, done everything they asked of him, and brought in shedloads of money. It seemed incredible that they wouldn't give him the salary raise they themselves had initiated. At the same time, he'd met Helen, and they were a good couple. Adam came from a hard-drinking South African background, and he needed a steady life, with regularity and security, and he was getting that and more with Helen. Also, he had a good job to go on to: the motoring industry in 2006 was still at full throttle, and the magazine world was far less stressful – and better paid – than newspapers. To be honest, it looked like he'd won the jackpot. We weren't to know that a financial collapse was imminent, that the motoring trade would fundamentally change as the market migrated online, leaving magazines such as *Auto Italia* as redundant as the dodo, and that concerns about the environment would finally force the industry to consider abandoning the internal combustion engine.

The industry had relied on oil-burning engines for more than 100 years and the emissions they generated was the source of pollution on a scale that had started to cause serious alarm in the 1960s, when the state of California had passed the first laws restricting CO_2 emissions from automobiles. By 2007, it was impossible to ignore the damage human beings were causing the planet.

Over years at the coal face, Adam and I had become best buddies and there was no way that was going to end overnight, but there was a huge gap in my working life after Adam left the paper, and I wasn't sure I wanted to stay. Little did I know that I was but half-way through my shift, and little did we know what was in store for us and the trade we had joined, a trade that had a proud history, with traditions forged over more than a century of serving communities.

– Chapter 19 –

The financial crash changed everything. The banks had flirted with disaster for years, and when they lost the plot, they had to be bailed out. This hurt the British economy and, for those industries vulnerable to internet-based competition, the danger was great indeed. This included the music industry, the car industry, retail, books, clothes, you name it.

In the print media sector, Facebook and Google had become a duopoly, taking something like 80 per cent of all digital advertising revenue between them: the newspaper world's total digital revenue stream, from all publishers, amounted to less than five per cent of the total advertising pot. Newspapers tried to extract revenue from their online model via subscription models, setting up paywalls and other registration procedures, but the take-up rate was alarmingly low: if a paywall went up, readers simply went elsewhere to find their news, to a site that was free. There was no cross-party discussion: at no point did the idea of an industry-wide payment model even make it onto an agenda. Every paper was siloed in like it was Stalingrad in 1942.

The individual newspaper groups were mostly owned by big conglomerates or by media barons who had their own agendas. They didn't trust each other. The idea that they could sit down and have a sensible conversation about the future of their industry was laughable. We're not talking about the regional press here, so much as the national titles. Newspaper owners have always been a breed apart: with Murdoch and Maxwell they'd become increasingly malevolent, tyrannical and cynical. Other publishing empires were opponents: there was never a moment in the last 50 years when they would have rallied together against a common threat. It wasn't ideology, it was ego. Every newspaper proprietor wanted to make Citizen Kane look like a lightweight and, to prove it, engaged in a continual war of attrition against rivals and potential rivals.

For a long time, until it was nearly fatal, they didn't understand that the internet was a rival: for them it was just a distraction. Then, when they saw the take-up, they prepared to see it off in time-honoured fashion, just like they'd seen off other rivals: to make cuts and dig deep until the threat was extinguished. This became the industry's fixed, indeed only, strategy from the early noughties. Rupert Murdoch at the *Times* and the *Sun*, Richard Desmond at the *Express*, the Barclay brothers at the *Telegraph*, the Rothermeres at the *Mail*... not having bought any of their newspapers for years, all I can say is that reading their online content is usually dispiriting. These proprietors have caused significant damage to the news industry, nor should it ignored that they all stash their money offshore while their titles promote a version of Britishness apparently that could easily have been invented in a Russian troll factory. The ferocity of these magnates' strategy has changed journalism, and not in a good way. No one watches the way they milk the country they purport to serve – because their titles divert their attention towards easy targets like the homeless, immigrants, movie stars, models, sports and all the others trapped in the bubble of fame.

The budget cuts started in earnest in 2007/8. The economy was floundering after the financial crash, and all sorts of unpleasantness could be rolled out with the official line of "due to the state of the economy the group has no option but to make cuts, and as a result of this....". How much of all this was done in a panic is hard to say, but some of it was opportunism.

At the *News*, there was concern but not yet alarm. Sales of the daily paper, which stood at around 47,000 a day in the mid-1990s, were now down to the 28,000 or so by the mid-noughties, but the financial success of the weekly papers at the *News* was apparently sufficient to ensure the Iliffe family would be happy enough, at least for the moment.

To start with, it wasn't so much cuts but changes. Murray Morse was either fired or quit: he seemed to have had some sort of difference with the managing director one Friday morning and was gone by 2pm. (By the way, if everything of significance seems to occur on a Friday morning, that's because the rest of the week was too frenetic to deal with anything much other than meeting deadlines.)

Murray was clapped out. I don't mean he was exhausted – this was a man of considerable energy – I mean the whole newsroom stood and clapped when he left, and banged their desks in time-honoured fashion, until he was right out to the car park. Right to when he drove away he could hear the thumping and the applause. He was liked (not that I was one of his biggest fans) because he'd trusted his journalists to do the job. He backed his team under fire. He wanted to try new things, but apparently they weren't the sort of things that Cambridge liked – as the group of concerned city burghers who had petitioned against "the tabloid road" pointed out. Sure Murray jazzed things up, with tabloid-style splashes, but that was a good thing and even if some folks were a bit freaked out it meant people were reading the paper and discussing its contents, which is all you want as a journalist. I call it the "pub test". When I walk in to the Old Spring what will my chums Tom, Tony, Patrick, Ben, Joanne, Paul and the rest be discussing? On that rating all was going well – we had their attention – but the circulation slide was unrelenting. Back then, whatever the circumstances, it was always the editor's fault if circulation dipped, though it was starting to become apparent that no one editor could change the technological straitjacket the industry was locking itself into.

In many ways Murray was one of the good guys. He was the news editor on the Scottish paper the *Daily Record* when the Dunblane tragedy took place: 13 children lost their lives to a mad gunman in a school that day, and Murray's report of the day's events, still available on the site for the press trade paper *Hold The Front Page*, shows that he was a reporter of the highest order. Whatever his managerial weaknesses may or may not have been he was a superb journalist. Management isn't my bag but good luck to those who give it a try: journalism is often badly paid, and anyone with ambition had to move away from the pit face towards the executive classes, even though the skills that make someone a good journalist don't automatically mean he will be a good manager.

It was six months before Murray was replaced. During that time deputy editor John Deex took over as acting editor. Everyone liked John, and was determined to make it work. That it did work was a testament to the professionalism of the team: if there was a problem, we realised John would prefer for us to solve it, so we learned to do just that. Being able to do this was an eye-opener: it heralded in a flat management style which was like releasing caged animals into the wild. If I had a problem with one of the weeklies, all I had to do was walk across the newsroom to where Nigel Brookes sat at the head of a team of six weekly newspaper editors (Nigel had moved sideways from his role as chief sub-editor), and explain the issue, and keep talking until a solution emerged. It was dreamtime: those six months of not having an editor were efficient, creative and productive.

It couldn't last, of course, and it didn't. Eventually the "new" editor was announced to be none other than Colin Grant: a safe pair of hands to management, an antidote to joy for the newsroom. Deexy left soon after to start a new life in Australia with his wife and family. We were back where we started.

Unfortunately Colin had a tendency to procrastinate which made him painful to work around, so you had to play along to some extent, and this trait hadn't gotten any better in his time away from the *News*. The inevitable result was that the levels of inertia became extremely irritating. The second coming of Colin was as much of a damp squib in terms of circulation as Murray Morse's reign, except that we had a lot less fun as Colin reimposed his unique style of management, but one good thing was noticeable in this period: there were a lot of overseas subs and reporters. Of the Australian subs Daniel Newell put in an immense shift for several years, and Sherine Conyers added some female Aussie humour to proceedings. A very smart Zimbabwean, Nomalanga Moyo, was on the subs desk, and the huge entertaining Mark McKissock on the sports desk was from New Zealand. A Canadian, Doug Gloin, who'd been a war reporter in South

America, also joined the fray: it was a colourful period in the newspaper's illustrious history. It had been colourful before of course, thanks to the Welsh wizardry of Randall Butt, and the Scottish contingent that began with Jock Gillespie on the health desk and went on to include Raymond Brown, the paper's most successful-ever crime reporter, a Glaswegian with the best nose for a story you'd ever meet. But they were home-grown, and the new internationalism chimed well with the times.

One day a new sub called Chris Marling came over to introduce himself. He was chatting to the sports editor, Paul Stimpson, and Paul asked him where he was from. It turned out Paul was from Pinner and Chris was from Harrow, which is my home town. I couldn't resist turning around in my chair and asking: "Which part of Harrow?"

"I don't think you would know it," said Chris.

"Try me."

"South Harrow?"

"Really, that's where I'm from!"

"Where's that?"

"Park Lane."

"Near the Tithe Farm?"

"That's the one…"

It turned out that his dad did regular gardening work for my mum: it was a surreal moment, and we've had a few laughs about it in the pub over the years, in a thick-as-thieves sort of fashion. Chris felt like an instant comrade: he clearly thought the *News* was a madhouse and didn't stay all that long, and went to work for a local digital marketing agency, so he's still around. Cambridge is a great city for ex-Londoners!

The recurring narrative of how to adapt my skill set – partly as a means to survive, partly as a means to offset the boredom that constantly seemed to be lapping on the shores of a restless mind – came into play again at around this time.

I'd become dispirited by computer games in the 80s, and was starting to feel shackled in the car trade. The motoring supplement went from a team of two to a team of six and then fell back to one. Adam had left, and Rodney had had to retire completely. Our very classy designer, Michelle Tovell, left for pastures new. It's always sad when talent walks away, but newsroom teams were being shrunk and it was better they left on their own terms. Freelancers were cut out of the equation too, which meant the motoring supplement had no more columnists like Ollie Batts, a former mechanic and a great observer of human nature, and no more PC Paul Stubbings, who was one in the sequence of highly literate local road traffic officers who posted brilliant reports from the front line of the automotive armageddon that was the A14. Although PC Stubbings wasn't asked to leave – not by us, at least.

The post of road traffic officer was made redundant by the local constabulary during the 'austerity' years after the financial crash. In an era characterised by short-sightedness, the call stood out as one of the worst because, without a road traffic officer on the roads, accidents take longer to sort out and are more expensive in terms of delays getting the injured to hospital. That was a wretched loss, though fortunately the post was revived after a few years as the value of the road traffic officers' role became obvious. Which, of course, was exactly what the front line officers predicted would happen...

In any case my interest it was dispiriting to be losing so many people and facets of the business. It meant more work, of course, and that started taking its toll. It didn't help that we were being asked to spend and increasing amount of time in meetings. Sitting in meeting rooms was taking up so much time that it was becoming a struggle to meet deadlines. Something, as they say, had to give.

The history of business management goes way back to the 18th century, when firms were run on tradition and instinct. As workforces grew, a new type of manager emerged and, to gain credibility, they used metrics borrowed from science to assess the performance of their employees. Scientific management aimed to maximise the productive capacity of each worker, which initially involved stopwatches and rulers, but by the 1970s things were changing and a new type of management-speak was starting to emerge, one which borrowed new-age concepts and elevated buzzwords into mantras which fluffed up the corporate handbook with phrases such as "thinking outside the box" and "blue sky thinking". And this torrid phraseology was followed by "touch base", "game changer", "ecosystem" and "going forward". And more – lots, lots more.

The problem was these phrases were being churned out by people who didn't actually have proper jobs: their job was to make "the machine" run more efficiently. To keep their jobs, they had to come up with reasons to justify their existence, and so they cranked up on management-speak and brought in a new range of tests and spurious metrics. One managing director insisted that we all complete a test to find out what colour our personality was: the test showed if you were blue, green, yellow or red. Blue was smart, green was creative, yellow was …. It was all absolute tosh, and some management consultant made a packet for sure, but it wasted a lot of production time.

Management mania for its own sake reached new heights at the BBC in the 1990s, when the then director general John Birt introduced a new "internal market" and every activity from the time spent doing an outside broadcast to the time spent cleaning the toilets was traded using a complex mechanism which naturally required a great number of accountants to monitor. Pretty soon the number of accountants required meant that people making radio and TV shows had to be laid off. The accountants only cared for their own employment, they had no loyalty or even interest in the work the firm was doing, their main ambition was to survive and grow the organisational side of things, and if that meant getting rid of the people who did the actual work…. What did they care? My younger sister Frances is a teacher: she is obliged to spend a significant chunk of her day satisfying bureaucrats who measure her performance down to the smallest detail, and she has less and less time to teach. Our education system has worsened with performance indicators such as those imposed by Ofsted (the Office for Standards in Education, Children's Services and Skills), because the institution gears towards scoring highly on the tests, and the joy of education is obliged to take second place, which may be why so many teachers are looking to work in a more meaningful profession. But even the more 'meaningful' professions such as doctors, nurses and GPs all have to defer to what Jenny called "the bean counters".

One anthropologist, David Graeber, says there is a reason for the rise in the use of management bullshit. He says that the West has outsourced production to other continents and that's left people with very little to do, but this new layer in the employment market keeps people in work even if it's not a necessary function. The people doing the work proper are actually carrying these new avatars of metrics, but the playing field is tilted so it looks like it's the other way round.

I was becoming less productive because of the number of meetings I was expected to attend and decided to talk to my GP about it. She listened closely to the description of the malaise from which I professed to suffer and then said: "I understand your concerns about your workload and the stresses that you are being subjected to, but what can I do?"

"You know I have a history of claustrophobia because I can't get in an airplane, I think that's on my medical record?"

Dr Leckie studied me closely. She had smiling Irish eyes, and I could never tell what she was really thinking.

"The thing is," I continued, "I actually have issues with being in meetings as well because I don't like confined spaces. I get very anxious and then start freaking out, so it would be in everyone's interests for me to not have to go to meetings. Would it be possible for you to sign me off from attending meetings due to claustrophobia please? They could just send me an email afterwards to tell me what happened."

Of course I was trying it on, but in a way this was a very cheap treatment, with no downside to the taxpayer. I would be happier and more productive if I didn't have to spend a third of the day in meetings. The treatment would cost the state nothing and cost my employers nothing. Even so, I was still gobsmacked when she wrote me out an exemption from meetings on medical grounds.

The next day I took the doctor's note in to work and left it on my line manager's desk. I was a meetings-free zone: when I told my colleagues they were hysterical with laughter and rage. Why couldn't they do the same? You couldn't make up the amount of respect and awe I got from this one bit of paper. The fact is, meetings are mostly bullshit, largely irrelevant and certainly a huge waste of time. Everyone knows this but it's hard to evade groupthink in a corporate setting. That doctor's exemption note was a trick I was proud to bring to the party.

All the same, the exemption only obliged me to focus even more sharply on my working situation. As the reach of the internet expanded, the motoring supplement started going down in size, from 32 to 28 to 24 to 20 and even down to 16 pages. It was a worry: I started wondering what else I could turn my hand to. The bald fact was that I was also not a genuinely great motoring writer: I was competent, but it was a masquerade. Maybe others didn't know it, but my best friends did and, more to the point, I did. However, I had successfully transitioned from a sub-editor to a sometime writer. So what else could I turn my hand to?

One day, in 2008, I was sitting at my desk when the business editor, Jenny Chapman, went upstairs to attend a meeting in the boardroom. When she came back she was in a bit of a tizz. I asked her what had happened.

"They want to start a business magazine," she said, "and they want me to be the editor."

"Wow," I said, "that's great, congratulations. What's the problem?"

"There's no budget," Jenny replied. "No budget, they don't want to pay me any more, and they don't want to spend any money to get it going."

"Oh dear," I said, puzzled. "That's tricky. Is there anything I can do to help?"

Jenny had a pile of books on her desk which I hadn't noticed until she slid them towards me.

"Well," she said, "it would be great if you could do some book reviews."

I accepted without, I have to say, any great sense of enthusiasm. But I was curious and when I got the books home and started poring over them it was a whole different story. There were some very interesting reads because the imbalances in the financial system were apparent for all to see after the banks' bail-out. One author listed all the bullshit trades the financial services industry had created, from sub-prime mortgages to bundled packages of junk bonds. Another explained how the financial crisis was the result of a testosterone imbalance in young men. Some politicians and business figures tried to explain how it wasn't their fault – they were clearly rattled. It seemed the financial crisis was all the fault of a greedy few "others", or was the result of an institutionalised and relentless capital grab by a few financial institutions and their wealthy backers, or was the logical outcome of neoliberalism… I discovered in 2010 that austerity was the wrong answer to the stuttering economy:

the right answer was to invest in rebuilding infrastructure and education for the next generation, because austerity would cause the economy to seize up. Other authors pointed to the accumulation of capital stashed in unknown accounts offshore, a practice the Nazis had started with stolen art money placed in secure Swiss trusts. Sixty years later, dozens of other jurisdictions had even more relaxed arrangements than Switzerland, which meant that businessmen and wealthy individuals were mixing with arms dealers and drug cartels in tax havens around the world, creating a whole new economic landscape that ordinary people were cut out of.

They do say that financial crashes bring opportunities and here, at last, was a chance to get my teeth into something that didn't involve following in someone else's footsteps. If it meant becoming a disaster capitalism journalist, so be it. The business world was changing as fast as the internet developed, and the new technology was helping take the whole show into some troubled waters. Those were the waters any journalist would want to swim or sail in, which would take me beyond the comedy carnage of computer games, beyond the wittering of the motoring backwoodsmen, into a brave new world and a series of economic, political and ethical situations that were entirely without precedent.

For that moment, surrounded by economics books, I felt like a pig in shit, and it was a warm and soothing feeling to discover that I had an "access all areas" card to investigate the causes and outcomes of the financial crisis.

– Chapter 20 –

Cambridge Business magazine started as a quarterly, then became a bi-monthly, then a monthly, within a period of two years.

Jenny rose to the challenge by calling on her extensive contacts to chip in articles and regular columns: pretty soon the cream of Cambridge's business cadre was engaged. Even Mike Lynch, the founder of Autonomy who had sold the company to Hewlett Packard for £7.4 billion in 2011, produced a regular column.

The magazine's design, initially set up by Martin Howlett, was subsequently expertly redrafted by long-time *News* sports sub-editor Andy Ormiston, who craftily and elegantly repurposed himself as a magazine designer.

For years, Andy had sat on the sports desk located on the next block of desks in the newsroom. Jenny called them "Druids", these sports guys: a closed order that worked together and spoke in a mystical language indecipherable to ordinary mortals. Many of them were "lifers": men – there was one female sub-editor, Judy, in 20 years of sports desk-watching – in it for the long haul.

Randall Butt was the chief football writer at the time of the move to Milton in 1997. He was a colourful writer and great office personality, a Welshman who carried grudges and jests like joker cards to be distributed evenly throughout the workplace. The local football team, Cambridge United, was a reasonably successful professional football club. I'd watched a few games with Charlie when he was a youngster, and though the squad boasted a lot of enthusiasm without too much skill, Randall was a brilliant live wire of a reporter, and his copy made every game riveting. After he left the sports section inevitably became a bit lacklustre for a while and it didn't help Randall's replacement, Aaron Mason, one bit when "the U's" were relegated to the next league down, which was non-professional. Aaron and his fellow sports colleague Mark Taylor had arrived in Cambridge together from a local paper in Swindon, and they fitted neatly into the new set-up. The U's crowd stayed loyal, but everyone knew it would be a big ask to get out of the sporting and financial doldrums the club was mired in. For a regional newspaper, having a successful local sporting club makes a big difference in circulation.

Andy was in the crew laying the sports pages out, and was known for sitting immobilised at his desk for hours without moving – not to make a cup of tea, not for a cigarette break, nothing. These stints could go on for hours and were really impressive in a sort of Buddha-like fashion. Every few months Andy would have an epic tantrum and it was as well to keep out of his way when these occurred because he had a collection of sports manuals – plus a row of Tolkien hardbacks – on his desk and you might see one flying around. But these occasional episodes were understandable because the sports desk was all blokes and they had to let off steam somehow, and Andy was an authentic legend and I was actually a bit awestruck by him. He'd been at the paper since the year dot and he was a lot of things I was never going to be: constant where I was fickle, steadfast where I was pliable, and upfront where I sat on fences.

One thing I did notice about the sports crew was that, although they apparently had a credo to ride together, there was no tea round on the desk. After we'd left the Newmarket Road site we had a kitchen/breakout room with a kettle to make tea and coffee. The general idea was that each department did their own tea or coffee round – sports, reporters, features, business/motoring and the subs desk. But no one on the sports desk ever took part in the ritual. I asked Andy why this was one time while he was having lunch in the rest room.

"Because we don't like each other," was his blunt reply. The words were troubling but there was mirth in his eyes… maybe.

To get on the wrong side of Andy would be like annoying an angry bear, but one of the things about working on *Cambridge Business* – and arguably the reason for its success – was that it obliged a bunch of mavericks to work together, and one thing mavericks have in common is the knowledge they're permanently drinking in last-chance saloon: everyone is one mis-step from oblivion. It was going to be hard going being in the same team as Andy, but I knew it was a crucial relationship and I was determined to make it succeed. Fortunately Andy had been on the sports desk for decades, so when he got his break into magazines he needed to make it work too.

Being caught up in Andy's slipstream would mean a long and horrible mangling so it was front foot all the way, which meant delivering the copy on time with interesting photographs and lots of potential for a creative design to keep him happy. This actually helped me raise my game still further so from that point of view it was a very productive period. The bizmag team already had a solid backstory, and all I had to do was keep on keeping on, while he had his work cut out building on a promising start. Staying on point involved a lot of graft. I sent my copy to Andy via email and then walked across the newsroom to the design hub to check he had enough photographs. Our only hope was that he would rise to the challenge, otherwise we'd collapse in an orgy of bitterness and recrimination. Fortunately he was well up to the task. His designs sang, every time. I grew to like him more as time went by too. He could still be a complete thug at times but I was no better. He was a Spurs fan, a mild exercise in self-harm if ever there was one, so it was all about making allowances.

Being the books reviewer for the business magazine involved a lengthy apprenticeship on the job. I felt like an imposter who could be unmasked at any moment, even though in a 30-year career (minus those years in Glastonbury) I'd never been the cause of any litigation, and no editor had ever had to issue an apology for what I'd written – as per those "Correction" apologies you see from time to time, saying "we got it wrong when we said such-and-such, apologies to those concerned". I'd started off in the computer games market, already an unusual route for a regional journalist. I'd pretty much been busking it all the way but now the bit was finally between my teeth.

It would be completely inconceivable for anyone with my background to make it in newspapers today. Many would say I was lucky to have gone from the subs desk to motoring editor, and they would be correct. To suddenly change course and attempt to reformat myself, a motoring journalist, into a business writer was audacious to the point of criminal stupidity. To pull it off, I had to work harder than I'd ever worked in my life. Business writing wasn't part of my day job, and I had to do both the reading and the writing from home, which was still a family home, with the brood moving through the gears of the education system. Around this time the girls had finished at university: Em had gone to Liverpool and was now back in Cambridge, and Flo had completed an international development course at Sussex and was living and working for a local humanitarian organisation. Charlie had a lot of chums and was out much of the time, but I liked his pals bigly and his goodwill was priceless.

Winters were spent reading about new forms of electronic currency, 'trickle-down' economics, entrepreneurship, genetics, the pharmaceutical industry, the effects of technology on employment and culture, the Cambridge phenomenon, the post-capitalist era and business ethics – a very rounded education which built substantially on the Economics A-level I'd acquired at school. Back then economics was a much more basic study of Keynesian policies, with supply and demand the only metric, and perhaps a smattering of GDP data. After the Iraq war in 2003 neoliberalism really seemed to be calling the shots, so I read a lot about the way capitalism had morphed, or been morphed, into neoliberal doctrine.

Had our society totally surrendered to neoliberalism? As always, it became a matter of finding out the origins of this doctrine, which lay in the Vietnam War in the 1960s. The war was getting bogged down in the second half of the decade and, during Richard Nixon's 1969-1974 presidency, then National Security Advisor (later US Secretary of State) Henry Kissinger decided to illegally bomb Cambodia, where numerous Viet Cong were based. The template was established. Back then it was called realpolitik – politics executed for practical rather than moral or ethical reasons. This meant making decisions based on longer-term outcomes and green-lighted the way for neoliberalism, so it was okay to overlook the fact that the short-term consequences of your economic activity might involve huge environmental damage, economic ruin and enforced poverty for millions of people. If it got your own interests over the line that was all that mattered. Such thinking had never been considered before, but the merging of political and economic influence proved irresistible to a new group of thinkers. At the centre of it all was a low-taxation economic policy which resulted in diminished public services (including healthcare and education), reduced workers rights, deregulation and privatisation.

We knew all about Henry Kissinger, of course, and realpolitik, and how Margaret Thatcher had adopted this thinking in the UK during the 1980s, but the project seemed to be benign until the new century dawned.

The unravelling of society's basic strictures began in earnest post-9/11. The 2001 attack on New York's Twin Towers at the start of the George W Bush administration (2001 to 2009) created an opportunity to ramp up the armaments industry and its associates, co-opting political discourse and sidelining concerned voices as it did so. Key corporates profited to such an extent that you could legitimately say they were looting the state. Bush's sidekicks, Dick Cheney and Donald Rumsfeld, built political and economic fiefdoms unlike any since the days of Ancient Rome, or the Borgias in Renaissance Italy.

The Iraq War, 2003 to 2011, saw the US government disgorge $138 billion of taxpayers' money into US corporations: ten contractors got 52 per cent of that cash. One, Halliburton, whose former CEO was Dick Cheney, received $39.5 billion through its Houston-based spin-off energy-focused engineering and construction firm, KBR. Often, the cash from these deals was handed out without any bidding process from competing organisations, nor was there any accountability as to how it was spent. Neoliberalism meant transferring wealth – public money – into the hands of private enterprises.

The transfer of wealth was also on a par with events in Russia after the collapse of Communism in 1991, when the oligarchs got hold of the levers of the state and set up their own empires, before Vladimir Putin restored some sort of control when he became President of the Russian Federation in 1999. How Cheney and Rumsfield must have looked across to Moscow and envied its leaders' ability to exploit its own people. Of course, after decades of Communism, Russia didn't have as much wealth as America. America's coffers were full before the Iraq war. Afterwards, it was downhill all the way, and America's power diminished to the point where 15 years later Putin could affect the outcome of a US presidential election with apparent impunity.

The financial crisis of 2007/8 saw the global financial system come close to economic meltdown and resulted in a fundamental shift as globalisation ceded ground to parochialism, nativism and xenophobia. Not that anyone told the markets: within two years it was business as usual for them and pretty soon after that the bonus culture was back to full speed ahead. The tab for the crisis was footed by the taxpayer. Politicians in the West introduced a programme of economic austerity which was soon abandoned by most nations and the EU, except in Britain.

The practice of "disaster capitalism" entered the lexicon. Disaster capitalism made money out of chaos: massive shocks to the system resulted in anarchy, fear and confusion, and in the process the pieces of the economy could be reassembled into a new configuration.

During the chaos and the enforced impoverishment that followed the financial crisis, trillions of dollars was siphoned away from nation states into offshore trusts, where it did nothing but mock the inequality that had opened up since capital controls were abandoned in the 1990s. All the dogs of war were let off the leash and it was going to be a bumpy ride.

One morning in 2011 Jenny called in sick. She phoned to let me know, having informed the editor as was protocol. But could I do something for her? She had spent months arranging an interview with the head of CSR plc, a semiconductor firm which was on the way to a billion-dollar market capitalisation – the second in Cambridge after chip designer Arm, which had emerged out of the chaos of Acorn Computers, makers of the BBC Micro which had kick-started the computer coding era in schools around the land back in the 1980s, overtaking Clive Sinclair's home computer revolution. Could I do the CSR interview in her place?

Minutes later I was calling the office of CSR's boss Joep van Beurden to explain the situation. It was 11ish and I was due there in an hour, so I rejigged all my other work in two minutes flat and started googling in a desperate effort to discern what sort of questions to ask. Everyone has a different interview style but mine is to have an A4 pad and a couple of biros. I don't record anything on a gadget so I am entirely beholden to the notes, and after the chat I reread the notes and consider the narrative possibilities they contain. People who theorise about good work practice forget that at the coal face of your working day it's all about expediency, how to get the job done in the most efficient way, and some of that would ordinarily be trial and error, but you can't afford to make any errors – linguistic, legal or factual – when you're a journalist. I've received no formal journalistic training, but if someone were to insist that I get some qualifications, I would go to my nearest circus and ask them how do I get to be a high-wire trapeze artist. You make your own rules when it comes to your writing style, that's why I can't stand the idea of journalism college.

The CSR interview went well. Joep turned out to be from the Netherlands, a country I was more aware of since Flo had started going out with a rather delightful Dutchman, Thijs. Flo's work in the development sector meant I was becoming more aware of how some firms in the Netherlands and Germany were pushing technological boundaries in, for instance, solar power. I liked Joep from the start, he took his time and was gracious and expansive throughout. There's no interviewee I've met who I haven't liked by the end of an hour in their company, but it's usually better if you can get a good connection from the off.

The CSR article went over well and a couple of months after that a similar situation arose with the head of Arm at the time, Warren East. Arm is one of the greatest firms ever to emerge from Cambridge, with a business model which involves designing chips which are used in computers and in 98 per cent of the world's smartphones. At the time they were designing 96 per cent of all the chips used in the mobile phones of the day. They still do, having added AI and the IoT chip designs to their portfolio. (Arm was bought by Japanese firm SoftBank in 2016 after a £24 billion deal master-minded by founder and global investor Masayoshi Son.)

When it came to Cambridge innovation I had a low-key connection. Arm had emerged from Acorn Computers, and at Micro Dealer in the 1980s we were buying from their subsidiary, Acornsoft, who developed and sold games and educational software, including language courses, software writing courses, teaching aids and the like.

Acorn had been formed in 1978 when Chris Curry left Clive Sinclair and teamed up with Hermann Hauser. Hauser was a smart cookie, an Austrian who had a professorial air and who built up an incredible portfolio of investments and skills. In 1980 Acorn made a computer to BBC specifications for use in schools as part of the Beeb's Computer Literacy Project. In 1982 the government's Micros in Schools scheme was launched, with a TV programme which involved Acorn's computer, and its success was assured. However, later in the same decade Acorn overextended itself in its bid to conquer

America and went through various contortions before effectively expiring by the time the decade was out.

While these latter-day shenanigans were going on, Acorn's two chief designers, Roger Wilson and Steve Thurber, were becoming chip designers, and were toying with 32-bit RISC (reduced instruction set computer) chips, even as Acorn was still officially on 8-bit technology, which was slower and more energy-intensive.

Wilson and Thurber went on to develop Arm's first processors, but Wilson did not become part of the Arm team when it was split off from Acorn in 1990 because Roger was going through the challenging process of becoming Sophie.

The big gaming success on the BBC micro in the mid-1980s, by the way, had been *Elite*, which was produced by Frontier Software, which remains Cambridge-based and is still run by *Elite*'s creator, David Braben. Cambridge's back catalogue is like the Beatles' – still making serious money decades later.

– Chapter 21 –

I was doing ever more for *Cambridge Business* magazine as the noughties were coming to an end. I was managing because my increased business workload coincided with the decline of the motoring supplement as the car market's migration to the internet became a stampede.

It was the same for commercial features: there were fewer pages to lay out. People could now Google 'florist', and read reviews of a firm's service, prices, location, news updates and contact details with a couple of clicks on their computer and that meant newspapers lost their primacy. Same for cars. Mediation between the customer and the provider was no longer needed: the internet was a democratising development in that sense without doubt, but it spelled doom for markets that failed to, or could not, adapt.

The same story recurs with new technology because turning swords into ploughshares is a challenge for the sword industry until it finds a way to adapt its skills towards making more efficient ways of tilling the land.

My line manager during this time was the chief sub-editor, Clare Turner. For a few years the firm had an annual assessment procedure, called 'the appraisal'. The appraisal involved sitting in a room once a year and talking through what was happening with your job, whether you were getting enough training, whether your chair was comfortable, and whether there was anything you needed to perform your job better. You sat in the room until you'd agreed a text about the state of play. Sometimes you'd wrangle over the wording while Clare, despite being ludicrously – and wonderfully – potty-mouthed, got everything formalised into corporate-speak on paper. Then you both signed it, and that was it.

For a number of years Clare and I worked on these formal statements rather quickly, and then she'd sit back and say: "Ok, so that's the nonsense out of the way, tell me how it's going with the bizmag hot sausage." Clare was funny: she talked like that to everyone. Gobby and quick-thinking, she was a great line manager and it showed how fast things were changing that she could occupy a relatively senior position for many years. And I'd say: "Well, it's pretty crazy but it seems to be working, and I'd like to keep going with it." She clearly thought I was bonkers but was decent enough not to try and talk me out of it.

The mountain, of course, was getting ever higher to climb. When people realise that something startling is being produced in a publication, they grab the next edition and expect the same heights to be scaled and then surpassed. The bar goes ever higher, and over time you go from being the disruptor to being the new target for disruption. People are watching to see what you do next, so you try and come up with something that will surprise and delight them. It's difficult in any marketplace to continually raise the bar, but Cambridge has an astonishing knowledge economy bolted on to its academic facilities and you don't have to look very far for very long before you'll come across something mind-boggling.

Gradually a business role that had started out as a book reviewer morphed into that of a feature writer, and I was invited to the monthly meetings with the advertising team,

Emily and then Tilly, plus the advertising director, Jonathan Tewson, alongside the design and distribution teams. To do this I set aside my doctor's exemption from meetings, but only temporarily: I still declined – much to the continued amusement of everyone who knew about the ruse – to attend all others except one-on-ones with my line manager. But the workload was rising to ludicrous levels again, and something had to give. With Jenny's okay I decided to drop the book reviews, but the decision wasn't based solely on time factors, it was also about the direction the content was taking.

Two or three years after the financial crisis and the search for answers had boiled down to business as usual. The Blair-Brown New Labour project was rejected at the ballot box and a new Conservative/Liberal Democrat coalition took power in 2010. The economic solution to the crisis was deemed to be more austerity, with the central idea being that savings – cuts – had to be made to recoup the losses the banks had made, and those savings would come from reducing state expenditure. Of course cuts are not the answer because they lower incomes, decrease economic activity and create a downward productivity spiral, so most nations abandoned the austerity project pretty quickly when they realised it meant that people stopped buying things and more people were being put out of work.

The UK government, however, locked on to the policy. Even though economists including Cambridge Judge Business School's Ha-Joon Chang suggested that austerity was the wrong answer to the issues thrown up by the financial crisis, austerity went unchallenged for five years, and was continued with greater thrust when the

Conservatives won the 2015 election outright. Chang was not alone in making it clear that best strategy is to invest in infrastructure, which creates jobs and keeps the wheels of the economy from stalling. Austerity trashed the UK's productivity and revealed some terrible and possibly fatal flaws in the democratic process as it did so. The social contract was weakened as the UK pursued the illusory rewards of a reduced deficit, and the despair and anger that the process generated would be mis-deployed against the EU just a few years later. But the Conservative party had a plan which was in action before the smoke and mirrors of the financial crisis had cleared. There's money to be made out of crashes.

"Balancing the books was not really what was behind this austerity policy," says Ha-Joon Chang of this period. "It was an attempt to undermine the welfare state, rewrite the social contract and re-engineer the British economy in the image of the American free-market system."

But writing about these issues on a regular basis for *Cambridge Business* was starting to feel like banging my head against a brick wall. The books I was being asked to review revealed a huge a mismatch between the policy and the problem it was supposed to address, but to go on about it was a hiding to nothing. Raging against austerity was feeling like gesture politics, as futile as King Canute trying to stop the waves. No one wants to become a one-note party piece, and a disgruntled and unhappy journalist is not an attractive proposition for readers, unless you're called Peter Hitchens. Fortunately Jenny liked the suggestions for the new sections that we discussed, and the resulting profiles of people and their work showed what an incredibly vibrant and multi-faceted Cambridge is. Some interviewees were craftsmen continuing the finer traditions of the city: sign writers, organ restorers and charity workers. Some were more prosaic: the front-of-house bloke at the city's central Post Office, a market stall holder. There were also interviews with scientists who knew how to extract the DNA from a mouse and replace it with human DNA so they could do tests on human tissue without an actual human being involved. I guess the common thread was that they were all creative in their own way.

It was fun to do these features, but the difficulty with producing a magazine housed in a newspaper environment is that while the two seem similar – both involve putting words and images on paper, packaging it up and putting it on sale – they are very different cultures. The timescales involved oblige you to dance to very different rhythms. The newspaper world is largely driven by adrenalin and deadlines, while magazines – a monthly has one deadline a month – can afford to be more cerebral. Likewise the advertising and distribution teams. They needed to think in big-picture terms, not just locally. Could we get the magazine into the City of London, or into airports? Jenny pushed hard for that, and I pushed hard for a cover price, because we were handing it out for free and *Cambridge Business* contained valuable market data about one of the globe's most fertile hubs. But asking a newspaper firm to adapt to the needs of a magazine is like asking a footballer to become a swimmer: both are sports, but the techniques involved are pretty alien to each other.

Cambridge is one of the world's tech and pharma hotspots, a city that, it's generally agreed, has been at the heart of the nation's economic recovery following years of austerity. In some ways the city had a relatively easy time during the austerity years because the local economy – which also boasts a vibrant tourist sector – was growing by 2 to 3 per cent every year, resulting in high employment levels and offsetting the fiscal carnage that was taking place elsewhere. The city's business hub was also slotting neatly into global demand for tech and pharma. This springboard was a very empowering platform for a business magazine and we had positioned ourselves rather well in this fast-developing economic hotspot – so well, in fact, that it was read, discussed and profitable even without a serious budget or proper staffing arrangements.

However, the problem was that if Cambridge as a whole had elegantly positioned itself to reap the benefits of the fast-developing technological age, the print sector, by comparison, was apparently falling by the wayside.

The critical moment in this new AD – the transition from analogue to digital – came right at the start, before the ubiquity of the world wide web, when the journalistic cadre was given to assume that although the contents of the newspaper would be available on the internet free of charge, the "free" model was temporary. By "temporary" we assumed a year or two. Five years would have been considered unthinkable, but what is it now... 15 years? Yes, we were informed that we'd scale up the amount of editorial content that appeared online and, as our website gained traction, an economic model would kick in. It wasn't clear exactly what economic model it would be, but generally it was assumed it would be something to do with paywalls.

Unfortunately, subscription paywalls have never really taken off to the extent required. They're unattractive because they imply a commitment that people don't necessarily want to make. Yes I like the *Telegraph* or *The Times*, but what if I only read the sports section on a Sunday? It's bad business to ask sports readers to buy into the whole paper for a month in that situation. "Really," thinks the browser, "I can find sports results and commentary elsewhere on the internet." The nature of an inquisitive mind is that it will find ways to go round problems.

The subscription model hasn't worked out too well for the newspaper industry because it doesn't give the customer what the customer wants and, as they say, the customer is always right. If I go into a clothes shop to buy a shirt and the salesperson is saying you can only buy a shirt if you buy a suit as well, I'll go elsewhere.

The industry has attempted to impose its preferred payment model on the internet and the online community has indicated that only a minority will pay annual or monthly fees. Yet, rather than adapting the model, the trade has just carried on with the offer regardless. The music industry had a similar dilemma a decade or so ago, until it adapted to downloads and then streaming services. So why is a subscription paywall model the only offer for newspapers? What if, when someone clicks on a story, they pay a very small amount just for that story? After all, the reader has registered an interest in that story, so why not ask them to pay a small amount to access it? The more research I did, the more it made sense, and eventually I came up with the PaperClick model.

The PaperClick model – which can't be fully explained here for commercial reasons – is about valuing journalism rather than being in thrall to the internet per se. Journalists and journalism are the reason that people go to newspaper websites. They don't go for adverts, they don't go for pop-ups. Yet journalists are conspicuous by their absence when it comes to sharing the plunder. Adverts, pop-ups and other intrusions are tolerated up to a point, but ad blockers are increasingly deployed to avoid seeing them.

During discussions to put a pay-per-article option together it's struck me how delighted the payment firms are that a solution might be in sight. They can see how good it would be for the newspaper industry. The telling component they most welcome is that the proposed model satisfies an immediate curiosity or impulse for information. If I see a story about Edward Snowden or an exposé of tax havens I want to read it. For others, it might be finding out about Donald Trump's latest Twitter rant and its after-effects, or what your favourite movie star is up to. At this point you're in "pay now, worry later" mode. There's a compulsive element to news which hasn't been factored in to any of the models. News is addictive – as any underpaid and overworked journo will tell you. Hopefully the PaperClick app will emerge at some point, though for sure it won't happen unless the industry wants it to.

Regardless of which model is finally successful, it hasn't helped that the newspaper market – which put it about that a solution was just around the corner for more than a decade and a half – didn't have a coherent payment model in mind at the start of the internet era, and since then decided to dig deep and hope to somehow ride the downturn out. You could call it the head-in-sand strategy.

The unfortunate outcome of this strategy is that internet giants like Google and Amazon have achieved far higher market valuations in a very short timespan, which allows them to invest a lot in R&D which keeps moving the game on. By contrast, the newspaper trade invests almost nothing in R&D. Never has because it's never seen the need to.

This isn't about blaming the trade: the news business is just one of the victims of a 21st century calamity-in-the-making. This calamity is hurting all Western economies and while the internet age has amplified it, its origins weren't in the digital age. It started with the Thatcher/Reagan years in the 1980s, when Western populations were first encouraged to consider themselves as consumer societies rather than manufacturing societies. Manufacturing was shipped out to India, Africa and Asia. We were lured into believing that we could all live on the "never-never", as my mum called it, forever. Politicians loved this new twist on the "you can have your cake and eat it" theme. Consumer rights became all-important and workers' rights were put on the backburner, resulting in a massive shift in the tectonic plates of the workplace. The technology of the 21st century is adapted to the whims of the consumer market because that was the market most receptive to their techno-wares. Wasn't that the idea?

The internet has accelerated the era of over-consumption, but in doing so it has harvested economies in the way Richard Branson harvests companies. The digital era has introduced a whole new global marketplace without any sort of by-you-leave or analysis of good and bad outcomes. Right back at the start of the internet in the late 1990s, the public was told that the internet was an amazing new free resource, and after a few years the notion of stuff being free or at least unbelievably cheap opened up a reality deficit. As consumers we soon wanted – expected – stuff like flights or information or connectivity or music for nothing or next-to-nothing. The way the product or service is brought to you, and how it's created, is barely considered. The problems come because most consumers are also workers, and workers expect to get paid properly for their efforts. How can they get paid if it's given away for free, or when the real cost is vastly discounted? This reality gap has created the mentality that has allowed workers' pay and conditions to be eroded.

You could say that if stuff costs less, then that makes up for stagnant wages, yeah? That works up to a point, but there's a reality gap there too: stuff only *looks* like it's cheaper. If I can fly to Barcelona for the price of a taxi from Cambridge to London (which often takes longer to get to than does the flight to Catalonia), why not? Cheap air flight is a wonderful thing, it has opened up horizons for millions, but the price of the flight doesn't include a CO_2 tax for the pollution, or decent wages for ground staff and service providers. If I buy clothes from Primark, that locks workers in Bangladesh or China into a system that any other era would call slavery, even if the alternative is zero income. What's the right thing to do? We all know the answer, but we're not ready to complete the circle just yet somehow.

Closer to home, the knock-on effects of the stand-off between the rights of workers and the rights of consumers are already apparent. Employees pay the price in terms of losing their annual wage increase, their salaries fall with inflation, pensions are binned along with sick pay rights and holiday allowances, and everyone is working longer hours and getting more stressed out. And still, no one questions the status quo. The suggestion that it suits some parties to focus public opinion on the rights of consumers in order to avoid close scrutiny of what is happening to the rights of workers has yet to shape the argument.

People in so-called advanced countries have opted for a separation wall between their actions as a consumer and their activity as a worker, and the refusal to link the two has suspended the basic rule of economic activity, that you get what you pay for. In the 21st century, a new group of consumers firmly believes that you get what you don't pay for, and a re-educational plan is urgently needed to disabuse them of this notion because without a value system, we are a lost cause.

Of course any payment model for internet content has risks – people may turn away, go elsewhere. Once you give something away for free, naturally people will resent paying for it. But what was it Thomas Jefferson said? "An educated citizenry is a vital prerequisite for our survival as a free people." You might look at it another way: "An uneducated citizenry is a vital prerequisite for our demise as a free people."

The divide between the rights and responsibilities of workers and consumers obviates citizens from the responsibilities that accrue to them as a result of their transactions, and society as a whole has been complicit in failing to point out the disparity. Soon, the artificial intelligence era will be upon us, and once developed it will be irreversible. The final demise of the workforce as jobs are taken over by machines will turn us for the most part into only consumers. Is that what we want?

Music, films, newspapers, information, social media, books have all had to redefine themselves online, with varying degrees of success. It's nice to have something for free – a film, say. And yes, the fact that you can find a site that will allow you to download movies without payment seems pretty cool. What's not to like? Personally, I don't know anyone who works in the film industry, so maybe I can not feel too troubled that someone somewhere might lose work because of my decision to watch their film without paying for it. People can massage their consciences any which way because they see people succeeding precisely because they appear to have no conscience or ethical DNA to encumber them, and they think: "Well if they can get away with it, why can't I?". The less conscience you have the richer you'll be, is how this particular deck seems to be stacked, but it isn't working and it never can work in the long term.

The journalists who carried on believing that the internet would pay out some day got it wrong too, and so did the strategists who put out the mantra that the industry's future lay in the digital arena. As journalists we acted in good faith, believing them, only slowly appreciating that there was nothing to back up these claims.

By 2010, the newspaper industry was clearly in big trouble. New, disruptive companies like Facebook and Google were making vast profits from online advertising revenue:

Facebook's 2016 ad revenue was $26 billion. New contenders like Twitter, WhatsApp and Snapchat were also seeing almost vertical growth while other, more traditional, industries struggled to rejig their offering. The music industry, for instance, made lots of money from records and CDs before digital: back then, going on tour was generally a loss leader. By ramping up ticket prices and merchandising opportunities as music sales shifted online, going on tour became more profitable to the point that it didn't matter so quite so much that artists didn't make so much money from downloads or streaming because their live shows did so well in terms of ticket prices, branding and revenue from merchandising clothes, CDs, mugs, jewellery, gadgets and the rest. That's a rejigged offering which has been relatively successful in adapting to a loss of revenue. A failing revenue source was offset by beefing up the offering in another.

The news sector, by contrast, failed to pivot in the same way. There was little sign of a plan B, which perhaps suggested no real intention to adapt. The only game in town was deemed to be a free online read, and a low-scale print edition which had a cover price or was free and paid for by print advertisers. Yet the figures didn't nearly stack up. Digital advertising revenue remained low: at the *Cambridge News,* even when print sales slid to 16,000 copies a day – a third of what they had been in the mid-1990s – more than four-fifths of newspaper ad revenues still came from print. Print may have been written off as the past, but it wasn't actually past it.

There were attempts to change of course, but with minimal or no investment. Reporters were expected to adapt to the technology by doing broadcasts or interviews to camera, but there was no training on how to do work in front of a microphone instead of a word processor. You just had to get on with the job, except it was in a different medium. Everyone expected the medium to adapt to newspapers, but when it didn't work out too well it was bunker down and ride it out.

No business can sustain the sort of hits the newspaper industry was enduring without taking action. There were two possible choices: either find a way to make money out of the internet – and quickly – or start cutting overheads. With no coherent revenue model on the horizon after nearly ten years of the internet, the axe came out. And down it came. In the 26 years since 1990 (the dawn of the internet age), 60 per cent of US journalists lost their jobs. It meant 458,000 journalists with jobs in the US in 1990 going down to 183,000 by 2016. The picture in the UK is pretty similar.

Yes, employment in internet publishing and online broadcasting rose from 30,000 to 198,000 in the same period, but that was never going to make up the shortfall.

In the wider economy, UK businesses were able to present cutbacks as an austerity measure, part of the fallout of the financial crash: indeed they were austerity measures, but the measures seemed only applied so far up the food chain. At the very top there was a vast amount of growth in terms of executive salaries and shares, and the way the residual rewards were steered towards shareholders didn't match the dogma everyone else was expected to chew down on.

Eventually the big picture emerged: between 1979 and 2007, household income in the top 1 per cent grew by 275 per cent compared to just 18 per cent growth in the bottom fifth of households. Ordinary people were all being taken for a ride downtown and the destination after that was poverty-ville: still these politicians were voted in, the kind that tried to blame the poor and the weak for what was happening to them, for being too fat or too foreign or too demanding – anything to distract attention while they scooped away the economic wealth that had taken generations to build up.

– Chapter 22 –

The churn in journalism is always considerable. Regional newspapers are a traditional access route to one of the nationals in London, and dozens of people came through the door over the years. It helps that Cambridge is less than an hour away by train from the capital, and being an international city of learning with one of the world's top universities on your doorstep helps too. People came to work at the *Cambridge Evening News* from all corners of the globe: good people and occasionally indifferent people, but the overall effect was hugely positive.

After Adam left, I'd get assistance from one of the subs, who would read pages, but all the subs assumed that knowledge of the car market was a prerequisite to working on a motoring supplement and decided en masse that they weren't up to the task. One described the Renault Espace people carrier as a "troop carrier". That's suggests a lack of common sense as well as zero knowledge of cars, but he went on to get and hold down a long-term role with a very respected economics magazine in the heart of London. A political correspondent became a Parliamentary correspondent. Another, a bloke who was almost mute – either from inclination or disdain, I could never work out which – went on to be a long-term sub-editor at the *Guardian*. One sports reporter retrained and became a successful lawyer, another went to work for the *Daily Mail* and ended up at the *Sun*. A New Zealander left to work at a top Sydney design studio. One sub became a stand-up comedian. Murray Morse, after he was "let go" by the *News*, went on to edit the *Daily Sport* and Robert Satchwell became director of the Society of Editors, a role he carried out with great aplomb for many years.

Back at the coal face the churn didn't seem so different, but the underlying rules were changing. When someone left they maybe wouldn't be replaced, and their role was absorbed by the rest of the team, but it was understandable – sales were falling, we weren't a charity. Supply and demand, and all that.

It hurt being on the back foot: our library was gradually wound down because cuttings from the paper were no longer essential. The stories were always there on the internet now, easy to find and available at the click of a button. The company's fleet of cars was sold off. Cars were leased instead, so the garage and workshop on the site were closed, meaning the excellent Polish mechanic lost his job and the transport manager, Stuart Mitchell, had to reinvent his role. Stuart wasn't made redundant though: he was an army man, and no messing. He was a logistics wizard and the Iliffe family was well known for liking longevity in its workforce, which they rewarded with a watch-presenting ceremony and a sit-down dinner with Lord Iliffe when you made it to the hallowed "21" club, established for those who had worked for the firm for 21 years. It was a proper Mapping & Webb carriage clock, too, and if you got to work for Lord Iliffe for 40 years you got a gold watch. It can't have been was easy to steer the company through these troubled waters. No one who builds a company over generations can enjoy managing a period of decline.

Stuart survived, but he was a changed man as he started to realise that the carnage around him, even though it wouldn't claim him personally, might eventually shake the foundations of the paper he had started to work for after leaving the armed forces in the 1950s.

At some point the drivers of the distribution vans went on to short-term contracts: eventually they were "let go" of too, and the distribution of the paper was handed over to outside courier firms. The number of print workers was reduced. The kiosks in the centre of Cambridge were shut down too. The kiosks were staffed by old guys who had maybe worked for the paper, or maybe were retired, or maybe they just needed the work. They were in their boxes selling the *Cambridge Evening News* in all weathers, but it wasn't just the paper they were selling: it was the brand. They were our front-of-house crew, reminding people that this was a community paper. Of course they were uneconomic as sales slid, and it was understood that the old model was being broken up but there wasn't a new model to replace it, but when the kiosks were shut we lost our ambassadors on the street. The reality was that there just weren't enough customers to make kiosks worthwhile any more.

There was churn at management level too. The managing director when I started at the paper, Ian Richards, was an enduring figure at the top. He was an old Navy man, I really liked him, and so did everyone else. He was always interested in you and your wellbeing, however high or low you were on the ladder. The fact that he would stop if you met him in the company car park and ask how you were getting on meant the world to me. It felt good to be working with such a man running the show. You felt you could tell him your problems. I mean you didn't actually do that, not one bit, but you felt you could. He was like a Gandalf, and if that's the Glastafari in me speaking so be it. You know those squaddies in the First World War who went over the tops of their trenches into the machine gun fire? That's the bar for leadership: would you do that for the firm you work for? If not, you're in the wrong job: move on.

After Ian Richards, the MDs were a mixed bunch. The one who was in charge during the Murray Morse era, Graham Ayres, went off to head up Weatherbys, the famous Wellingborough-based racing organisation which also had a presence in Newmarket, ten miles down the road. It was James Weatherby who, in 1791, published the first volume of the General Stud Book, a comprehensive register of all thoroughbreds, which is still published today. Graham, an accountant by trade, was replaced by Mike Richardson, an unusually gregarious man for the role. Mike handed over the development of the business magazine to one of his chums, Paul Gibson, who seemed entirely out of his depth with the team of misfit but not misfiring nutters – and the beautifully elegant advertising executives, Emily Lloyd-Ruck and Tilly Macdonald – he was tasked to lead. Gibson disappeared soon after his boss left.

Richardson was a shooting star. He was a wild card. He was best remembered in the newsroom for attempting to install astroturf to the entire office. He said: "You're all players in a team, you should be playing on astroturf!" He seemed entirely serious: we heard about the cost of it, which was phenomenal, more than £100,000. A projected date was made for the installation, but it never happened. Someone pulled the plug on the project, but it was a fun journey while it lasted.

At the top of the long-established company that owned Cambridge Newspapers was the Yattendon Group, which was run by Lord Iliffe. The Iliffe family had first owned the *News* in the pre-war period, sold it then bought it back a decade after the war. Robert Iliffe was liked and respected: the view was that he was surrounded by some pretty hard-headed men, but you need some nitty-gritty when you have a portfolio of harbours, property, TV stations and newspapers to run. He was once said to have called the *Cambridge Evening News* his "jewel in the crown". It was hard not to like a man like that, and you felt you didn't want to let him down. Gradually, he was handing over to his son, Edward, which meant a period of transition, thereby adding to the sense of uncertainty about the future, as any such handover is likely to be.

As it turned out Edward was perfectly capable of ensuring the company prospered, even in the difficult financial climate he inherited. Daily sales were continuing to slide but the group's overall profitability was very good, thanks to more print work and the fact that the weekly regional titles continued to make good money.

But the industry in the throes of significant change: web traffic, while growing, was still not delivering serious revenue, so the axe kept falling, and not just for us, this was across the industry. Various new methodologies were developed to keep the show on the road. Novel ways of distributing the paper for free were found. This bolstered circulation so that the relatively high print advertising rates could be justified. The tactic mostly involved delivering "bulk" copies to certain locations where they could be picked up for nothing. Giving away copies is a short-term measure, of course, and the gambit annoys paying customers but, until a better strategy was developed, tinkering at the edges of the problem was deemed the best that could be done.

My mission at this time was straightforward: a formal business role. I wanted something with "business" on my business card. It was getting irritating to say to the heads of some of the world's top firms "here's my card, sorry it says motoring editor, the stationery department hasn't caught up with my expanding role". Haha. The line was a busted flush. Did that make me a busted flush? Not yet, but pretty soon, if it didn't get sorted, the ruse would wear thin.

There were no noises that a new job description was coming my way. Jenny was calm personified but behind the scenes, over a bevy at the Old Spring, she was infuriated. Not only had they not given her a budget, drastically increased her workload and not offered her any more money, but they were making it hard for her biggest ally to contribute to the magazine for free. I didn't really mind. The important thing was that she let me write what I wanted in the style I wanted – indeed she insisted on it – and she saw off any naysayers. That was the silver lining. To be sure, she needed help to do her job too: she had a monthly magazine and a weekly newspaper supplement to produce on her own, and there were rumours of a daily page. I could write and do any production extras, like the proofing, to keep the show on the road. Plus I'd shown a stubborn streak that had been in danger of becoming self-destructive but could be used to advantage. You win more battles if you're prepared to outlast anyone who gets in the way.

As it became clearer that there was no imminent end in sight to the problem of falling revenues, more drastic action was required. At the end of 2012 it was announced at a formal company meeting that the subs desk was to be eliminated. The plan was that all sub-editors would have their jobs terminated and could either take early retirement, where applicable, or be reassessed for a smaller number of design and "content manager" roles.

Mary-Jane Carreyette and Keith Bailey decided to take the retirement option. One of the subs, Hannah Dunleavy, aghast at being effectively sacked then made to reapply for her own job (the "content manager" title was dismissed as a ruse), turned down a job offer and left without a redundancy cheque. Her decision seemed both brave and foolhardy at the same time: it was at the extreme end of the spectrum, but many toyed with the idea of calling it a day, if only for a second. Not me, of course: I had a family to feed.

Clare Turner was chief sub so her role was safe. Russell Vaughan, John Meredith and myself decided to pitch in for a content manager role, along with most of the design team, which meant resident design genius Manwai Wong was obliged to battle it out with superstar Vanessa Holmes, "safe pair of hands" Jim Elsegood and a couple of others.

The reassessment involved both the subs and the design teams going out to a conference centre near Bedford for a day and completing some layouts during a two-hour test, after which we would be interviewed by an independent team of employment advisors. The process began in November, but the outcome wasn't due to be announced until spring the following year. That was a fraught Christmas and new year for a lot of people.

But even before the drama of the disappearing subs desk had subsided, the concerns of the outside world had to be put on hold again as Cambridge Newspapers began a merger process which would result in the Iliffe family losing control of the paper, and coming close to losing its footing in the city for the first time in generations.

– Chapter 23 –

While all this drama went on, the city continued to thrive. The first human genome had been sequenced in 2003 – three thousand million base pairs that define a human entity were identified, one by one. The result was a massive acceleration in the field of genomics which the city was well placed to benefit from.

Over the years there have been some very smart people who found their natural habitat in Cambridge, starting with Sir Issac Newton in the late 17th century and running through to Professor Stephen Hawking. Newton discovered gravity and was voted the greatest Cantabrigian of all time in 2009. More recently, Francis Crick and James Watson discovered the double helix structure of DNA in 1953. You can still go along to the pub in which they celebrated their discovery, The Eagle, and look at the inscriptions carved into the woodwork of the time. Professor Hawking's legacy will also last centuries…

The discovery of DNA became the foundation for medical breakthroughs which facilitated cures for all sorts of disease. Genomics as a scientific field of study emerged from Crick and Watson's discovery, but it took a long time for the discovery of DNA to be of any use. If you were going to report on it you had to have a working knowledge of what the science entailed, which could pitch you unexpectedly into some of humanity's most profound discoveries.

Cambridge, a unique combination of an 800 year-old university town with a 21st century science park ethos, hit a purple patch in the 1970s and has never looked back. It started taking shape in the computer sector, but biopharma was moving into position as a global force to be reckoned with. Highly skilled investors such as Mike Lynch and Hermann Hauser added a new level of expertise to the hundreds of academics, entrepreneurs, engineers and medical experts who were contributing to the store of human knowledge in hugely practical ways. After Crick and Watson come other Cambridge-based Nobel prize winners including Frederick Sanger, Martin Evans, Elizabeth Blackburn, John Gurdon, Robert Evans and Joseph Stiglitz. World-class scientists including Sir Greg Winter and Sir Christopher Evans worked side-by-side with world-class bioscience entrepreneurs such as Darrin Disley and Jonathan Milner to develop the prestige and success of the city's bioscience sector.

The university came on board, backed by substantial wealth and land assets. Trinity College's Dr John Bradfield started the first Science Park in the early 1970s, underpinning the Cambridge phenomenon and nurturing an economic hub which was developing solutions to some of our species' greatest problems in energy, medicine and technology. Alongside the serious stuff came the computer games side, which was by now developing Virtual Reality headsets: big US firms opened new bases in Cambridge, including Microsoft and Sony. I was anxious when I did an interview with the lead at the Sony games studio in town. What was my connection with the computer games scene now? I found out when I walked in to Sony's studios to interview the chief designer and there was that week's copy of *Computer Trade Weekly* on the table in the foyer. It looked familiar, design-wise, to the product back when I'd been launch editor. That was poignant. I was the forgotten statesman to an industry I'd helped teach to walk.

There was a thriving independent games scene in the city too, with firms like Frontier – who had grown magnificently since the days of the BBC Micro and was still under the watchful eye of David Braben – and Jagex, the agile and hugely successful creators of the online game phenomenon that is the Runescape phenomenon. These guys had the cream of the world's software geniuses working for them.

To cap it all, one day I was walking through the centre of town and someone yelled "Mike!" from a car: it turned out to be Jeremy Cooke, Micro Dealer's international sales manager from back in the 1980s. Jeremy had stayed in the games sector and had his own games design firm. It was great to catch up and it cracked me up how much like Phil Collins he still was. "Look what we helped create!" is what I think when I see Jeremy.

Such an incredible city deserves incredible media to celebrate it, and *Cambridge News* was still delivering editorially, and not just on the business side either: the features team was celebrating another side of Cambridge – the food and artistic side, which was responding well to the ministrations of new ideas, themes and flavours from the street food and pop-up scene. But all the while the cracks were starting to become apparent. As the cost of homes spiralled towards unaffordable levels, two new banking terms were introduced: the bank of mum and dad, and the food bank.

People are naturally resilient. You can't solve the world's problems overnight, whichever pub you drink in, and it's natural to seek refuge from the tumult outside your door. In another generation it was fishing or bridge nights, now it was technology's turn. The smartphone was becoming ubiquitous – a 24/7, controlling, life-defining gadget, expanding in terms of features and quality at a phenomenal rate. Apple's first iPhone was released in 2007 and instantly revolutionised the mobile phone sector. At the start of the new decade – let's call it the teens – desktop computers were old hat: there was a range of android phones similar to the iPhone, fully internet-enabled, with vast amounts of memory, a camera, Bluetooth and pretty soon – after a slow start – there were apps to measure and enhance everything possible aspect of human activity.

Cracks like climate change and untrammelled financial greed and the endless "war on terror" could, however temporarily, be papered over or ignored as the excitement of the smartphone era began. Who has time to sit and ponder what the world might be like in 50 years' time when your inbox is overloading and you're only ever a click way from a post that will make all your friends admire and envy you? Today, 85 per cent of Americans get their news via their mobile phone, and 70 per cent of Americans use social media as their preferred news source.

Just a generation ago there were two daily news broadcasts on television, of around half an hour each. Now there are many 24-hour news channels and even if you can't even be bothered to go to a newspaper's website, you can read about what people are talking about on social media.

Where once you had to be organised to find the news, now you have to be organised if you want to opt out.

But new internet experiences haven't always been positive. Left to its own devices – literally! – the human imagination has actually shrunk even as technology has expanded its potential. Every other era in human history has turned its imagination up to full volume to find out about the outside world, whether it be from the stars or from the town crier, but now your imagination is being drowned in a huge tsunami of information your brain can't cope with, and your imagination is so saturated it doesn't work in the same way any more. Society conferred an instant legitimacy on Silicon Valley's offerings which are only now causing headaches. It's unrealistic to put the genie back in the bottle even if that were desirable, but it's surely reasonable to expect Google and YouTube not to publish images involving terrorism or pedophilia – and to pay taxes.

Just as newspapers queued up at the social media feeding trough, the Facebook community – 2.2 billion users by 2018 – started turning the volume down on newspapers' online offerings. Such users mostly seemed to want trivia. They log in to be distracted from current affairs, not to be reminded of them. Social media celebrated the individual and his or her friendship groups. Corporate offerings and branding messages look clunky in the fun house, and news spoils the impromptu party vibe. Shutting the news out permits users to slip into the familiar cocoons of groupthink and mutual brainwashing.

Most newspapers, including the *News*, engaged with social media platforms in a haphazard fashion. New digital roles were created – digital editors and digital traffic analysts, the avatars of the new science of analytics – but the people who performed these roles were posting content according to a formula and a schedule, and the whole point of the internet era was that it wasn't formulaic, it was about novelty. The *News*' online content was basically traffic woes, court cases and incidents in which the fire and/or police services were called out, dished up with a smattering of sports and perhaps the odd feature about food. Not so much on culture, not many reviews, and certainly not any political commentary, indeed hardly any commentary of any sort. There are very few columnists earning a living in regional newspapers.

Online, business content rarely got big hits. You could work half a morning on an article about a new cancer cure but a video about a controlled demolition of a building would scoop all the hits. I did video reports about cycling, local events and businesses, but the video that got me the biggest hits involved a crane that caused a hole in the road as it was being pulled into position.

The day-to-day advances in science and technology happening in Cambridge could as easily have been taking place on another planet in this new forum. Who knew who would work online? We were told that science and technology wasn't what people wanted to read about, but how did they knew that when this technology hadn't existed for long enough for any sort of data to be collated? In any case, the data that's collected shows only numbers: it doesn't show the value of the information to the reader. If you post a story about a charity fundraiser, it may only get a few clicks, but that's not to say readers won't see it and think: 'Oh, that was a good story about the local community, I like this paper, maybe I'll buy it next time'.

People are fickle anyway: at the most successful newspaper of the modern era, the *Daily Mail*, the astrology was, for a really long time, by far the most-read section. People want what people want, and if you don't offer it then someone else will, and in the new information era it was all up for grabs.

– Chapter 24 –

As the sub-editors renegotiated their roles with management towards the end of 2012, rumours of a takeover began. There was a new company being built to turn around the ailing regional newspaper model, a company formed of three existing news organisations: Trinity Mirror, the *Daily Mail*'s Northcliffe Media and Yattendon, the Iliffe family trust that owned Cambridge Newspapers among many other interests.

The new company, to be called Local World, involved Yattendon taking a 20 per cent stake and a seat on the board. The thinking was probably that economies of scale made sense for the firm at the time. By being part of a larger organisation costs and service such as IT and accounting could be spread. In stormy trading conditions, it made more sense to be part of a larger unit. Having a seat on the board meant Yattendon, with Edward Iliffe now fully at the helm, had a voice about what happened to Cambridge Newspapers. They were still printing the paper, and had a say in its future.

Local World was run by a former Trinity Mirror executive, David Montgomery. Montgomery was associated with some of the industry's most brazen plays and power grabs. He was an okay editor at the *News of the World* from 1982 to 1987 and went on to rise through the Murdoch ranks. In 1992 he took over as chief executive of the Mirror Group following the death of Robert Maxwell, and plunged the publisher into an era of doubt and uncertainty with savage cuts which brought shareholders a satisfactory return but substantially weakened the connection with readers: sales fell considerably.

In 1999 Montgomery left the Mirror, and went to work as a media mastermind specialising in mergers and acquisitions. His modus operandi was to buy businesses out and start a sell-off process disguised as restructuring, before a take-the-money-and-run exit two or three years later. He was the footballing equivalent of a big-ego hotshot international manager who achieved great results – not least in terms of his own pay scale – before moving on to a bigger club. His manner was that of a benign-but-busy autocrat. In 2005, during his takeover of the *Berliner Zeitung* newspaper, a German journalist wrote of Monty: "It is easy to form the impression he doesn't much take to the human race and the human race hasn't much taken to him."

The plans for Local World seemed to involve making promises to shareholders which couldn't possibly be delivered by raising advertising revenues and circulation: they could only come from job cuts and closures. Anyone could tell you – surely including the man himself – that his reign would mean deep job cuts and plenty of strife and difficult times.

So here we were, and it felt like being sold as cattle to an unknown new organisation magicked out of thin air. Would it prove to be an industrial abattoir or a lush new playing field? It didn't take long before we started worrying that we'd been on board a luxury liner that was now entering waters both unfamiliar and full of enemies – politicians who wanted to curb the power of the press as part of their own agendas, hustlers who wanted to buy newspapers for their own financial purposes, and a new breed of proprietor who wanted to turn newspapers into the mouthpieces of their owners. Some on board the great ship *Cambridge News* headed for the lifeboats. Others headed for the bar. A few sat on deck trying to see where the ship was heading.

The closure of the subs desk wasn't necessarily the end for my role or roles. The immediate concern was how to ride out the culls. Did I mention I had a family to feed? In effect I'd been both a writer and a sub-editor for a dozen years, but was still being paid solely as a sub-editor. I was in real trouble for sure because I wasn't a good enough page designer to be a full-time designer – I didn't know how to use Photoshop, for instance, the industry-standard design tool for doing picture cutouts. But then again, I could write headlines, which designers couldn't. Nor was I ideal content editor material: the production side of the job was fine, but what about the writing, was it an advantage that I could do both?

I was an anomaly and failed the interview to become a content manager in the new regime. So did Russell, and he was far better suited to the role than I'd ever be.

We were told that we'd be called in for an interview with our line manager to be given our leaving date. Many of the old hands departed: the majority on one Friday. Mass leaving days, that was a new one. By late spring of 2013 I still hadn't been called in by Clare Turner, so I went to the deputy chief sub, who was still (just) Hannah, and asked her what was going on.

"Look, Mike," she said. "They'll call you in when they have a leaving date for you. Until then, just carry on with your job."

So I carried on. After a while it seemed maybe I wasn't going to get a leaving date. A stay of execution had been granted, but for months I expected an exit interview any day. I never asked about Clare about the situation, though, didn't want to give her ideas. I was living on borrowed time, and I never found out what went on, but I'm pretty sure I was spared by an intervention from Jenny. I don't know what she did or said, but eventually a "commercial features content manager" role was found for me. Not just that, but when we were all asked to submit the wording for our new, Local World, business cards, I was told I could have "business writer" as part of my job title. The advertising director, Jonathan Tewson, always a positive influence during years of turmoil, was enthusiastic about the idea. But before that I had to have a meeting with the deputy editor, who wanted to be sure I didn't expect any more money in my wage slip. When he realised I didn't, my new job title became "Business writer, motoring editor and commercial features content manager". On the masthead of *Cambridge Business* my name came underneath Jenny's and read "Business writer".

It was late 2013: my two-year quest to develop a role on the business desk had turned into a five-year odyssey, and the result was all the sweeter for having overcome the odds mitigating against such a possibility. Computer games, motoring, and now business… it had been a slog, but I had pivoted without falling over. How, I'm not sure. If I knew, I'd be able to write one of those "How To…" books and make shedloads of money.

– Chapter 25 –

Being part of Local World meant Cambridge Newspapers was in a huge melting pot of regional newspapers across the UK.

The new group owned 16 daily newspapers, 36 paid-for weekly newspapers, 40 free weeklies and 63 websites. Everything would be administered centrally from Canary Wharf, where David Montgomery was based. The territories were carved up for a handful of managing directors who would report directly to him. The structure of Local World was slightly more vertiginous than its home: the gains of the flatter management style which had worked so well in the newsroom after the departure of Murray Morse were entirely torn up. Everything flowed into and out of David Montgomery's office, firstly to the managing directors, then down to management teams including editors, then down to the reporters, content mangers and photographers. We were cogs in a fiefdom.

There were some benefits. Each newsroom was obliged to adopt group structures, which meant a certain standardised computer architecture. To start with, the system was faster, but the in-house IT department was closed – "eliminated", to use the word du jour. The end of another era.

The early days of IT at *Cambridge News* involved a bloke called Gordon in a white laboratory coat wandering around the newsroom with a clipboard, taking notes of any issues before retreating to the IT lair, a small office near the lift where piles of old computers had piled up, with monitors, printers, keyboards, motherboards and leads all over the place. Gradually a service had been built up, headed at its very efficient best by Pat Hills, who was methodical and calm under fire. That's all you really want from an IT technician – the ability to withstand the heat of battle. When your computer crashes, or becomes unbearably slow, your working day starts to look like a mountain you'll never climb, and journalists start to crack under the strain of being left on the sidelines while everyone else is bringing home the bacon. Of course the problems got sorted eventually, but how long was anyone's guess. The main skills set required of an IT bloke – it always was a bloke – was to look knowledgeable and be a bit of a soothsayer. He was philosopher, priest, actor and geek. Technical knowledge was pretty secondary. Encouraging this crew to get the best out of elderly computers clogged up with years of computerised detritus was what we had to do, which was achieved by a combination of pleading, raging and, ultimately, entering a catatonic state from which it felt that no light would ever enter or escape, at which point your IT technician would finally be able to work without your constant interruptions.

Outside in the fag shed, it seemed these guys had too much time on their hands. One of the IT folks had discovered a porn site which had pictures of one of the female reporters and told all in the fag break. I was a bit shocked: I'd been out on a date with the reporter one time. A lot of the evening was spent discussing the Israeli-Palestinian conflict, if I recall correctly. She was smart and savvy: I wondered how the pictures got there. If someone posted them against her will that would cross some legal line, but it was also possible she put them online or allowed them to be put online and that was an error of judgement. Having porno pictures of her online would do her career no good at all, and I felt upset on her behalf. Perhaps needlessly: maybe she just thought it was a bit of fun.

Whether connected to this or not I don't know, but she left the firm and indeed the industry not long after, and it made me realise just how weird is the double standard for women in the workplace: men are the ones doing all the leering, but the woman's career suffers. Blokes allegedly aren't capable of concentrating if a woman arouses their desire and she cops the blame for their inability to control themselves. It makes the world go round, apparently, but there was only one instance where sexual harassment was reported at the *News* all the time I was there, and that was an obsessive type of situation – which outside the newsroom would have been called stalking – where the bloke wasn't getting the message, and he wised up pretty fast when he was given a cease-and-desist warning.

The ethos of the IT realm changed in the Local World era: fixing the slow or crashed system was outsourced to Bangalore, in southern India. The firm involved delivered computer care over the telephone, via a helpdesk open 24/7. The Bangalore team could take control of your computer and resolve most emergency issues, but there were any other matters, such as changing over computers, which required a permanent IT technician to be located on each site. This service worked quite well, although we quickly bypassed the official route of phoning Bangalore in favour of just knocking on the door of the IT office to resolve issues and pleading with the technician, then filling in the paperwork afterwards.

We quickly became dependent on the in-house technician, but couldn't get too cosy because they were changed over every year. Each had a one-year visa and returned to India after their year was up. Their wages were probably dreadful, but for these Indians – the first was Karthick, followed by Deepak and then Praddy – this was their first taste of the UK and, in a place like Cambridge, they found a very warm welcome for their skills.

Having spent time in India, and loving the people o the sub-continent, I was delighted to see them and wanted to help make their time in England a success. I knew they would probably talk about it for years: their grandchildren would probably get to hear of our antics. I made sure I was on my best behaviour when they came into the newsroom to fix my computer. In quieter moments I asked them where they were from: having been asked "Where are you coming from?" a million times on the sub-continent, it felt only fair. I asked them about their family, and how they had come to be working for the computer firm, and whether they liked Cambridge.

They all revealed relatively humble but proud heritages: it made me realise how much India was changing. In some ways they had landed in the promised Western nirvana, because Cambridge is a deeply civilised place, with a wealth of historic sites, but the counterpoint to the incredible city was the shambles they were witnessing around them. The newsroom must have made the babbling masses of the average Indian city seem like a pleasant afternoon listening to a church choir. On occasions the cacophony and confusion made the workplace resemble Dante's Inferno. The massed cohorts of people with all sorts of skill levels and needs, all clamouring for the IT guy to visit their desk, would have shocked even the most outrageous baba in all of Calcutta. This was not the England of cricket fields and warm beer, this was an England in the engine room of the new digital revolution, and there were people cracking up, suffering tortures and indignities both private and public, people watching their labour going the way of the dodo if it hadn't been saved properly... Everyone had times when it felt like they were going mad in the haste to adapt to new technology, and not all of them were going quietly. Your average IT technician needed advanced counselling skills, and it helped if he looked like a Bollywood philosopher. It made me happy that we had these guys in the newsroom helping us: sometimes it seemed they were the only normal people in the room.

The computer system IT installed and maintained was the same for all Local World titles and included a software change which all editorial staff were required to get to grips with. Quark XPress had been the industry standard for more than 20 years – I'd used version 1.0 when working for Chris Anderson in 1987 – but it was inflexible and was replaced by Atex's Content Manager system. The Atex system had long been in use in London: the infrastructure in regional newspapers was still a decade behind the curve, but when it finally arrived the new architecture was clearly more sophisticated. You could post stories online in Atex, for instance, which gave us a certain frisson of excitement until we realised how laborious and anti-intuitive the procedure was.

Such was the reach of the new digital technology that even the photographers had to change their working practices so they could send pictures electronically via add-ons to their cameras, even if these were already years old. The camera market was also going through the throes of change: the conventional camera was being outgunned by the cameras becoming standard on smartphones, which had incredible quality. The days of going into the office to drop off a roll of film to the darkroom, which had been run by Sandra Burkett since before I joined the firm, were over. Sandra took her retirement cue, to spend time with her grandchildren – the leaving formula involved either that or "to spend time in the garden".

When Sandra left the photographers effectively lost their anchor: there was no need for them to come into the office any more. Pretty soon there would be just one picture desk editor, which was a long-time core role, a key newsroom position which had always been the preserve of a gentleman, for that way the group of unruly mercenaries of which he was head would have a civilised face to the wider world. Cedric defined the template of courtly ringmaster, benevolent compere and a stickler when it came to his primary task, running the diary, which was a big ledger. When email arrived the paper forms for bookings were replaced an electronic equivalent and that little bit of personal interaction – delivering the form, to Cedric's desk in person – was lost.

After Cedric it was Eddie Collinson. Eddie was a lovely man, another one of those people who understood that his job only marginally involved balancing the needs of his photographers with those of the reporters. His main role was to endure with endless patience the antics of office life, and quietly get on with laying down the law through the magisterial control with which he spread the photographic workload out for the day and weeks ahead.

After Eddie the role was taken on for a while by Keith Heppell, a Yorkshireman who didn't take to the role, so after a year or so he went back to being a photographer which is what he enjoyed, and the new picture desk editor was our favourite Northerner, Dave Harwood, a football man (Manchester City) and a wonderful entertainer, famous for an incident that occurred when someone riled him – or was it because he was bored? – and he stood up on the filing cabinet, dropped his trousers and mooned at the whole office. I assume from the furore his behaviour caused that he dropped his pants (underwear, for American readers) and probably revealed a glimpse of ball sack as well as bum crack to boot. Bizarrely, I was sitting within ten feet of this wonderful (or grotesque, depending on your point of view) act of showmanship, and didn't notice a thing. I think I was becoming what would have been called a "swot" at school.

Dave was a great office entertainer but gradually the people were having to adapt to the technology where before it had been the other way round, and for the picture desk that gradually meant the diary was shared to everyone via an online document, which reporters and advertising teams could fill in.

It wasn't Dave's fault that his department was being reconditioned to fit the new technology: the same thing was happening everywhere. Rumour had it that reporters would be asked to take their smartphones with them when they went out, so they could take the pictures. They actually tried that on a couple of local papers up north, at which point they realised that perhaps taking photographs was actually a separate skill. They rowed back on the idea, but the point was made, no one was ringfenced, everyone was an endangered species, and what ended up happening was the same as everywhere else: fewer jobs, more workload as you suddenly had two mouths to feed: print and digital. The photographers went out to do a job, took pictures, then sorted out which ones to add to the photographic library, and none of it needed to involve being in the office.

Pretty quickly they got used to it: some said that was okay, they were happy enough to sit in a coffee shop and use the wi-fi there to access the computer system, the office wasn't too welcoming since they'd had their department desk taken away and the only photographer in the room with a desk was Dave, who was a people person, and it can't have been nice for him to not see his crew so much. People who left weren't replaced, which meant more and more jobs for those remaining, so in the end they didn't have time to come into the office. They were all really great folk, Warren Gunn, Keith, David Johnson, Richard Patterson and Keith 'Boxer' Jones were the final cadre. They were all good and sometimes great photographers but the pressure of having to be on a site and get photos done in 30 and sometimes 20 minutes meant that they didn't feel any respect was being given to their creativity. When Adam had started booking in cars to photograph locally for road tests, he'd take out a photographer and they would have two hours to do a sequence of pictures for a road test which might go in the paper or maybe in one of the magazines – two fashion/style magazines and the business mag were being produced. And even then, if you looked at a car magazine on sale at the newsagents, the photoshoots involved days being on-site, often in far-away locations.

Eventually those two-hour car shoots were condensed into half an hour and we'd not try anything too ambitious like filming the vehicle next to a punt station by the Cam, because you know, you'd get stuck in traffic, a warden would tell you to move on, passers-by would ask questions, and you'd end up wondering why you were bothering when you could just go round the corner to Milton Country Park and get all the shots in a wooded lay-by.

Everyone was being shunted through the hoops of the new technology without so much as a "by your leave". I'd seen this before, in the computer games era, but that sense of a step change had only lasted a couple of years at its most intense, this was ongoing and every day you were adapting to new geometry as the restless search for audience share went on.

Our Atex training lasted a morning and then we were left to get on with it. There were no slow content managers, being left behind was not an option, so everyone pulled together as much as possible and pooled knowledge and skills so people ended up doing something they were vaguely good at. If anyone couldn't work something out they could ask around, and you'd help if you could because sometime you'd need help and good knowledge sharing capabilities in both directions are a definite asset.

For instance, claiming expenses on the new system was so fiendishly fiddly and time-consuming that it was impossible not to think that this was to put people off from claiming at all. The laborious form-filling certainly put people off, but it was noticeable that there would always be someone who could help you with something technical, and a colleague would take any amount of time to show you how to do something you weren't sure about. We really were all in it together.

Some of the designers had incredible skills in this respect: when Atex came in they seemed to have been using it for years from day one. There is a collegiate component to working in a newsroom. Still, the fact that people were leaving and finding productive things to do in the outside world was inescapable. It made sense to keep your options open – I'd done shifts at the *Independent*, Jenny did some shifts on the *Daily Mail* business desk, Keith the photographer ran his own business selling specialist camera parts. When people made the leap you'd think 'good for them'. Down at the Old Spring on a Friday night, we'd toast them and share stories about their antics that made everyone chuckle. All in all I reckon we wrung a few laughs out of it all and it felt like we were the last ones continuing the journalistic tradition of chewing the fat at a regular pub on a Friday evening, where anyone and everyone was welcome.

In 2014 *Cambridge Business* was entered for a national award, the Santander Financial Media Awards. The bizmag was to win the title for Best Magazine three years in a row. The first two were as part of Local World, the third was under yet another new owner, Trinity Mirror.

– Chapter 26 –

Local World didn't last long: as was suspected, David Montgomery cashed out pretty quickly, it seemed at the earliest opportunity: any faster would have seemed like indecent haste. The brand existed for a mere three years.

Rumours started appearing in the national press about a possible new deal, and in the spring of 2016 it was announced that Local World was being acquired by Trinity Mirror in a £220m deal. The shared ownership model, involving the Mail group, Yattendon and Trinity Mirror, had run its course.

In its final year, 2014, Local World generated revenues of £221m, with £39m of "adjusted operating profits". The external perception – to the markets, to the shareholders – was that the regional print sector was emerging from the slump leaner and fitter. Progress was being made, and of course the suggestion – however subliminally – that the media sector was finding a way to shake the magic internet money tree was music to the ears of those who wanted it to be true.

The new deal saw Trinity Mirror, which had owned 40 per cent of Local World, paying £164m to buy the remaining shares, valuing Local World at £220m. But there was a twist: Trinity, according to *The Guardian*, "has agreed to sell a handful of titles in Cambridge and Hertfordshire to Edward Richard Iliffe, owner of Iliffe parent Yattendon Group, which holds a 21.3 per cent stake in Local World, for £15.8m".

The situation seemed pretty straightforward: Edward Iliffe had a seat on the board of Local World, and owned a handsome chunk of stock, and he would lose this if Trinity Mirror bought him out. By selling he would cede control of Cambridge Newspapers and his family would no longer have a voice in one of the UK's most prized cities. It seemed he didn't want that to happen, so a deal was negotiated for a buy-back.

This new plan was very intriguing for the workforces of the Cambridge and Hertfordshire titles. The Iliffe family wanted to buy their Cambridge titles back – they cared about us! We always wanted to believe it but now it was out there: we were worth fighting for. It tasted like victory. A fresh wind was blowing at last, and it wasn't hard to see the Iliffes as our savior, rescuing us from being swallowed up by a giant corporate fatberg.

The Yattendon proposal wasn't a sentimental one. The Iliffe family had built up a formidable legacy in Cambridge, and maybe there had been some sort of rethink: perhaps the benefits of being part of a larger group were outweighed by the disadvantages.

Cambridge is a unique city, where quality is respected and valued in a fast-moving global marketplace. In a huge public company's portfolio of regional newspapers, the needs of an individual city are liable to get lost.

If your average UK city is, say, Swindon, then some of the territories in the group will be doing a lot worse than Swindon, and some a lot better. Cambridge, suffice to say, would be doing a lot better – no disrespect to Swindon – so from our point of view we would rather have the rest of the group coming up to our standards of coverage, rather than have to dumb down to suit the average levels of quality across the group. Having an owner who understood and respected the local economy, and specifically intended to develop the business rather than remodel it in the Trinity Mirror mould, was always going to find a ready-made audience at the *Cambridge News* water cooler.

The plan to revert the titles to Iliffe seemed to be going well: in February of 2016 Edward Iliffe even came to the *News*' office to discuss what the company would look like after it came back under his control. His message was that, in an era of asset-stripping, he wanted to invest in the paper. He believed in the future of the company. There was no detail of precisely how the planned changeover would be managed, but there was a sense that a plan was in place. The Iliffe team looked good. At Lord Iliffe's side was former Cambridge Newspaper chairman David Fordham, a much-respected executive and excellent tough-but-fair negotiator.

Intriguingly, Fordham had been taken on by Trinity Mirror to act as their advisor. So if Trinity Mirror wanted to hire an Iliffe insider to shepherd the deal through, that surely meant they wanted the transition to go smoothly. Fordham knew the way Iliffe liked to work and would represent his views accurately in any discussions at Canary Wharf, and here he was, in the newsroom, touring the site and answering questions with a bit of a sparkle in his eyes. Could the good times come back? That was probably not in anyone's gift, but at least we could look forward to some investment and were actually respected by our owners. To be backed by people who actually like producing newspapers is a far better fate than having our futures weighed by curiosity-free bean counters who knew nothing about the trade or the local economy.

The rumour is that the deal was sealed with a handshake. Maybe it was along the lines of Trinity Mirror saying verbally "we'll recommend this deal to our shareholders". Maybe there was something in writing, who knows, but it didn't happen. At the last minute, in March 2016, it was announced via a stock market update that Trinity Mirror had acquired the Local World portfolio, and no mention was made of the Cambridge and Hertfordshire titles. Questions were asked about the omission, and then we found out: we were all going to become Trinity Mirror employees.

How the deal was scuppered became a bone of contention in the corridors of power, and a talking point in the newsroom. The pro-Trinity Mirror suggestion was that Iliffe had, perhaps accidentally, missed some Stock Exchange deadline to authorise the buy-back and Trinity Mirror had had no option but to go ahead because there wasn't any time for any sort of renegotiation, Trinity Mirror being a public company with shareholders to keep happy. The other view was that they simply decided they wanted to the keep control of the Cambridge and Hertfordshire titles after all.

Which theory best fits the facts was the question. It seemed difficult to conceive that Lord Iliffe, with a profound knowledge of English law and customs, would "miss" a vital Stock Market deadline. His professional advisors would surely be informed of such matters, and given ample time to get their paperwork formulated and submitted. Option B seemed much more likely. Trinity Mirror probably simply changed their minds about the sale.

"Cui bono?" is the question you have to follow in these instances – who benefits? "Follow the money" in plainspeak. Consider the Trinity Mirror position: they had newspapers in every region of England except East Anglia. Why would they let these East Anglian titles go? Maybe it helped that, of all regions in the country, Cambridge is best positioned for growth thanks to its booming local economy and global standing. Maybe that made no difference to them, but why had they changed their minds so late? Why had they encouraged Iliffe to believe that the deal was good to the point that it was officially announced? One option was incompetence, the other was some sort of late strategic rethink.

Whichever version was true – and it might have been a combination of the two theories, or another option that hasn't been identified – there was a clause in the discussions which meant that Trinity Mirror would pay Iliffe Media a one-off sum of £2 million should the buy-back not go through, and Trinity Mirror did indeed pay the £2m as stipulated in the contract which, probably as a bonus, may have also ensured that the details of the acquisition would never need to be examined too closely.

What happened next was even more surprising. Our editor of seven years, Paul Brackley, left.

Paul was news editor at one of Yattendon's Essex titles prior to being appointed to the editorship of the *Cambridge News*. Being made editor was quite a promotion, not least because he was still in his early thirties. No one knew what to expect, but he had been fast-tracked during the Colin Grant years, so he clearly had talent, because not much was fast-tracked in that era.

Every new editor is given a period of breathing space when he or she takes over at a title, and after the honeymoon period was over it was apparent that Paul was an absolute master of the system, knew the IT set-up way better than we did and was highly organised right from the off. That mattered a lot, because it meant he knew what was possible and what couldn't be achieved. For instance, I might have a run of commercial supplements to produce, and the gaps between them were vital, and the source of a lot of trench warfare with the advertising department, who wanted them produced for tomorrow's edition. I needed to know if I'd have a chance to get some sense restored to proceedings if I appealed to the editor, and I did.

Paul's editorship was notable for his extreme levels of technical competence and ferocious work rate. He had shunted the sometimes reluctant, often suspicious, newsroom through a bewildering variety of changes without any serious errors of judgement. And yet, despite following protocol and senior management instructions to the letter and indeed to the spirit of the letter, it suddenly seemed that perhaps he didn't want to take the newsroom in the direction Trinity Mirror wanted for the paper. Or was that reading too much into it?

I was on holiday the week he left. I'd done my handover for the motoring and commercial features production on the previous Friday. The bizmag workload wasn't factored in: it was spread over a month which made it more manageable, but there were still a lot of commercial and motoring pages to be done. All went well: "Have a good week off."

Mid-week I heard from Jenny that Paul was leaving on Friday. The circumstances were entirely opaque, with only the briefest of leaving officialese being followed. "We would like to thank Paul for all his hard work during the seven years of his editorship" was probably the most effusive comment issued by the company on the editor's exit. The traditional lunchtime drinks were to take place in a nearby pub in Milton, the Lion & Lamb, on the Friday, so I got suited and booted and cycled over to say goodbye. I'd become a cyclist after 2011, when I'd had a mini-financial meltdown which involved silly levels of credit card debt and sold my car. It was six years before I had another set of wheels other than the bike, and during this time cycling became second nature, not least for visits to the pub. It worked well: I'd not cycled since I was at prep school, but it was a joy. What settled it was that it wouldn't be very seemly for the local motoring editor to be done for drink-driving, so that was how I became the only motoring editor in the UK not to drive a car.

The Lion & Lamb was packed but there was a curiously muted feeling in the air. No one talked about the obvious: why was the editor leaving? It seemed probable that only Paul knew what had gone on behind the scenes, and this was not the time to raise such topics. He'd been a good editor in difficult times. I had a couple of beers and chatted with various colleagues. There was no speech. Before leaving I walked over to Paul.

"You off, Mike? Thanks for coming," he said.

"Yes. I just wanted to wish you all the best for whatever you do next," I said. Standard protocol. "And also I'd like to thank you for being so supportive to me."

Paul looked mildly quizzical at this: there had never been any obvious show of support, but to me support can take two forms – active and passive. I had received active support – I had been given the "business writer" moniker under Paul's editorship. That was the icing on the cake, but the passive support, of not standing in the way of my development at any of the key points, was of at least equal value.

"The fact is," I said, "you've never stood in my way and that has allowed me to develop my career at *Cambridge News*, and for that I'm very appreciative and I wish you every success in the future."

Paul looked extremely surprised that my gobby reputation had a nice side and then smiled. "No problem, Mike, thanks. I hope things work out well for you."

Job done. I'd actually managed to say what I wanted to say at the time it needed to be said. Not something I always achieve, along with many others, I suspect, in the writing trade. In fact I'd go so far as to say that people for whom the written word is crucial to their livelihood have particular difficulties in face-to-face situations. It's not the inability to find words that is a struggle, it's being aware of the myriad ways that language can be misconstrued and mis- or re-interpreted: talking can be like walking through a minefield. Precision is vital but the exchanges conversation brings tend to resemble a white-knuckle ride in a canoe through rapids. Usually it's a whole lot of fun, of course!

Being appropriate in the context of a situation isn't something taught in schools, and maybe it's a facet of common sense – "stating the bleeding obvious" – but there's no reason it shouldn't be acknowledged or discussed, especially in an entirely new era where kids from their early teens are expected to have mastered not just technology that would have defeated their great-grandparents, but the social skills to be able to juggle profiles and relationships on multiple different media platforms as well as what previous generations called "real life".

Hats off to them for being so damn good at it, but no one should be thinking it's easy or even natural.

– Chapter 27 –

Suddenly, in the summer of 2016, having lost control of Cambridge Newspapers in circumstances that must have been galling, the Iliffes faced a situation in which the family business had no published product in Cambridge for the first time in generations.

The *News* had originally been acquired in the 1920s. Now, nothing. Nada. Well, not quite nothing – there was a team of people around Edward Iliffe whose role was supposed to have been to run Cambridge Newspapers, headed up by managing director Ricky Allan, who had been an excellent and hugely popular advertising director at the *News*. There was the Iliffe printing press in Milton and a spare £2m recently deposited in the bank account courtesy of Trinity Mirror's compensation for having failed to let the *News* go. In such circumstances, wouldn't it cross your mind that, given you're set up to be a newspaper publisher, why not start a new one and get on with it?

The first question to be asked in such circumstances has to be the age-old "is there a gap in the market?". The answer was that even if there wasn't an obvious gap just yet, one was opening up. The mood music swirling around Trinity Mirror's plans for the Cambridge site was all about digital, possibly even digital-only. Print was being extincted, rather than dying of natural causes. It seemed plausible that print had a future in the same way as radio had a future after the arrival of TV. To abandon print for an internet-only model meant you'd be on the web with a million other digital-only titles: print has a cachet the web couldn't hope to replicate.

So would reinvigorating the print model be a good course of action? In a town like Cambridge, there are a lot of people with inquisitive minds and they are people who welcome serious, properly-researched content. If Trinity Mirror wanted to lead on digital-friendly content, wouldn't that leave many prospective readers unsatisfied? Maybe the digital-first route is the wrong emphasis for the longer term: in revenue terms, it was a gamble. The outcome wasn't clear in 2016 but the fact remained that, for most UK newspapers, two-thirds of revenue was still coming from print and only one-third from digital. Producing a paper with a cover price which had advertising revenue attached to it was still a successful financial formula. The UK market was leaner but millions of newspapers are still sold every day in the second decade of the 21st century.

So, in the thick of the newspaper industry's biggest remodelling since the arrival of double-sided high-speed presses in the 19th century, the Iliffe family went ahead with its plans to launch a new title, a weekly newspaper called the *Cambridge Independent* which, under the editorship of Paul Brackley, published its first edition in September 2016.

The arrival of the new paper wasn't entirely a bolt from the blue to us, because the offices of the two newspapers were located on the same site in Milton. Milton 1 was the print works which Iliffe owned – the very print works which continued to print the *Cambridge News*. Milton 2, a hundred yards away, was the newsroom, which was taken on by Trinity Mirror. But Milton 1 had office space as well as the print works, and that was where the new newsroom was to be located. The two company car parks were on one site which was then separated by a wire fence. It was partition time.

We were neighbours, but neighbours fall out sometimes and when that happens it can get ugly. The new product was of interest for its potential to disrupt sales, but it was a weekly rather than a daily, so not necessarily direct competition. That's just business life, but there was another concern – the possible appeal of the new title to *Cambridge News* staff who might be swayed into joining the new team. No one knew what the Trinity Mirror era would bring but it would certainly involve change, and the difficult aspect of change when it's managed from afar is that the local market, and the individual components of a newspaper that serves those markets, often get sidelined in the enthusiasm for "restructuring". What would happen next?

There was a long standoff while the rumours swirled. The next person to join the nascent title was the senior photographer, Keith Heppell, the phlegmatic Yorkshireman with a wry sense of humour who had his own take on working practices, most famously a tendency to ask questions of the people he was supposed to be photographing. One time I was at the AstraZeneca unveiling of their massive new site by Addenbrooke's Hospital, an event which attracted national coverage when the pharma giant announced its new HQ in Cambridge, and Keith spent half an hour talking to executives without sticking up his camera while I waited patiently beside him. Another time he asked the executive of a firm I was about to interview: "But isn't it true to say your technology is two years behind the curve?" I really wanted to stick his mouth over with packing tape, but I also wanted to laugh out loud, and it was difficult to contain both impulses. A brilliant question, for sure – just one that will lose you a lot of goodwill.

Asking whether you or your firm has lost the plot is a question all technology companies get asked because general knowledge struggles to keep up with this sort of scientific development. Alan Turing was probably asked it quite a lot as he considered computing and artificial intelligence's core dynamics, and Steve Jobs was certainly seen as a lunatic when he introduced the first Apple Mac. But that's Keith for you. He was always having a laugh, even if sometimes I just wished he'd stick to taking photographs, not least because his photographs were so bloody good.

Keith couldn't discuss what – if anything – he knew about the *Cambridge Independent* while he still worked at the *News* but the chief photographer, Dave Harwood, decided something was afoot and went on about it. "Went on" included questioning Keith's loyalty, sometimes to his face, but Keith brushed it all aside. One time I was reporting on a cycling event beside the river Cam which involved the local cycling organisation, CamCycle, and I asked Keith about the rumours of his batting for the "other side" – in terms of his employment, that is.

"The thing is, Michael," he replied, "I've got a mortgage to pay and you've got to look at what's happening at the *News* and ask: 'How long is that going to go on for?'"

It was an honest reply and when he went off on a riff about how the *News* was going to be sliced up and thrown to the dogs I could hear my mind going into denial mode. It'd been happening for years – the slicing and the denial – but at the time I wanted to believe Keith's judgement was off kilter. Later, I realised he'd shown a lot of gumption. People are taught they're safer in packs, and striking out on your own is brave.

Others also departed, including deputy editor Andy Veale, who'd been editor at the *Huntingdon Post* when I first met him at a car launch. Always good to meet someone for the first time over a drink, to be sure. Andy's seriously solid work rate made him a good person to work with and around, and it helped with his having a great newsman's sense of humour – bawdy, but never spiteful or uncharitable.

Some of the ad reps left to "go over the road" too. It was all getting a bit "man down". A couple of ad reps were escorted off the premises by the advertising manager when they handed in their resignation and said they were going to work for Iliffe. That wasn't nice to behold. Trying to strip someone of their dignity in the workplace is not a good look. I can't say I enjoyed working for Trinity Mirror too much, but maybe these antics weren't orchestrated by head office, maybe it was just local staff trying to impress their new bosses with how dedicated and loyal they were. That didn't work for me either though: loyalty is earned, you can't give it away in one go. If you try to swap your loyalty you have to ask yourself whether, from where you stood before, it looks like disloyalty.

Late in 2016 Trinity Mirror unveiled its "digital first" strategy which meant that editorial policy was now primarily directed towards online traffic. To achieve this stories had to be posted on the website as they were written, round the clock. The print edition would just become a selection of the best stories "tasted", or picked, by a separate print team. There were early shifts, late shifts and weekend shifts on the new rota.

In this new model print was an afterthought, publishing news that had already appeared on the website, sometimes 24 hours previously. Everyone knew the change was a gamble, because the revenue from digital was still a trickle, but the new owners wanted to believe it would work. In reality, it was just an exercise in groupthink, and the worst excesses of groupthink occur when there's a common enemy to unite you even closer. Then things go really guerrilla. It was a bad time and it got harder to stayed focused on the kind of quality the city deserved.

In November of 2016 I went with Jenny to the Santander Media Awards for the third and final time. Jenny was pretty convinced *Cambridge Business* wouldn't win again but the team was as strong as ever, and the magazine continued to benefit from world-class contributors from the local business community. After collecting the third SMEs Magazine of the Year title, Jenny announced in the taxi home: "We've achieved a hat-trick of wins, that's it, I'm not going to put us in for the next one." I dissented, but really I agreed: we'd probably sailed the good ship bizmag as far as we could. It was a poignant moment.

As the city continued its rapid expansion, premier-league Silicon Valley firms including Microsoft and Amazon set up shop, but there was always far more going on at ground level. Companies like Bango were building the online payment platforms used by PayPal and Amazon in the city, Darktrace was activating new possibilities of real-time cyber security, and Arm's chips were laying down roads to the next technological leaps in IoT and artificial intelligence. Engineers of all stripes emerged from the university to start up or work for these incredible corporations, and some of them would hive off and launch their own start-ups, and some of those would hit the jackpot with products and services no one else had conceived of.

On top of all this the pharma giant AstraZeneca announced it was moving its headquarters to Cambridge. The city was becoming such a business hot spot that we could have produced a weekly business magazine – if we had the staff and resources.

A hat-trick of wins seemed good enough for *Cambridge Business* magazine. To enter and not win would have been dispiriting: better to go out at the top.

– Chapter 28 –

After the first cull in 2012, which saw the subs desk closed, those who remained knew that though the axe had fallen elsewhere on that occasion, it would probably come back one day – and when it did it would be harder to fight off. But we carried on anyway, there was no sense of a tailing off, quite the contrary.

I learned during my time at Future Publishing that magazines have a certain trajectory, and from the off you need to hit the ground running and keep the momentum going for as long as possible. Positivity breeds positivity and you try and ride the bucking bronco of publishing with verve and tenacity. If there's a good team, with the advertising crew not just on board but enthusiastically on board, the distribution is solid and the management knows its chops, and you've got someone who takes ownership of the success of the project – in this case Jenny with me as her consigliere, fixer and cheerleader – then, well, let's just say that if there is an audience out there then you've got a chance of reaching it. So many things can go wrong that, when it does go right, you've got to keep pushing on as best you can. That's the plan.

Outside of this bubble thinking all sorts was going on. The new editor-in-chief was a former deputy editor of the *Liverpool Echo*, David Bartlett. He reported to Trinity Mirror directly, meaning the managing director had been outmanoeuvred and was now irrelevant. Jonathan Tewson, the ad director, left to work at Newmarket Racecourse. Jonathan's role was taken over by the *Cambridge News'* dead-man-walking managing director, which kept him safe for a while, but the new lot were merciless. A few months later he was ousted, to be replaced by a TM executive based out of London.

Bartlett had good credentials: he'd been on the right side of the Hillsborough inquiry, which had rumbled on in Liverpool for decades. Hillsborough was a football stadium in northern England where 96 football fans had died in a crowd crush on April 15, 1989 while attending an FA Cup semi-final game between Liverpool and Nottingham Forest. The subsequent inquest returned verdicts of accidental deaths, but there had been a cover-up of written records by some police officers on duty at the stadium that day which was concealed from the public and investigating agencies. As always, even worse than the cover-up were the lies that accompanied it. There were allegations of drunkenness among the fans and these allegations were reported by the media, and the *Sun* in particular.

The *Sun*'s coverage of the Hillsborough disaster included claims that Liverpool fans had picked the pockets of victims, attacked emergency service workers as they tried to help the injured and dying, and urinated on police helping at the scene. These incendiary claims, later debunked, constitute one of the darkest hours in newspaper history.

The coverage, as it later – much, much later – turned out, had largely been written by a Sheffield-based news agency, Whites, and it was the *Sun* wot run the Whites reports, almost verbatim. Whites later stated that one of their journalists had an unsolicited approach from four senior police officers immediately after the tragedy. The officers fed the reporters the stories. The paper said it had done all it could to corroborate what they'd been told before publishing.

But the reports were uncorroborated, and the decision by the *Sun*'s editor of the time, Kelvin MacKenzie, to lead on the story – under the headline "The Truth" – resulted in a boycott of the newspaper in the city. The boycott was estimated to have cost the newspaper's owners, News International, £15m a month for 28 years, and the coverage is often referred to as one of the greatest mistakes in newspaper publishing. But even so the cover-up held for so long there seemed to be no hope of the families getting the justice they deserved.

It was to *Liverpool Echo*'s credit that it flagged the story up consistently over the years before April 26, 2016, when the verdicts of accidental deaths for the 96 were overturned and re-rendered as "unlawfully killed". This was a complete vindication of the "Justice for the 96" campaign's hard slog over a quarter of a century, made the *Liverpool Echo* a good paper, and if it didn't automatically make David Bartlett a good editor then it certainly suggested he knew where his bread was buttered, because the media has a duty of care to its readership, and in Liverpool that duty of care was very relevant to the local community. Helping to overturn a huge wrongdoing was a good thing in anyone's book.

The early signs were promising and it wasn't David Bartlett's fault if the honeymoon didn't last long. He reported directly to the Trinity Mirror team, also in London's Canary Wharf, which ensured that there'd be no pleading in the negotiations between the newsroom and Trinity Mirror's diktats: there were no special arrangements for the jewel in the crown. At the same time, surely they wouldn't buy the

News only to make further cuts? Hadn't they fought hard to get us?

Any hope that there may be some sort of negotiation between London and Cambridge was futile. The editor was specifically there to impose Trinity Mirror's methods on the newsroom – fair enough, but there are degrees of imposition and this site's fate was going to be on the hard end of the spectrum.

The strategy for delivering a top-to-bottom newsroom revamp involves long-term goals and short-term goals.

In the longer term what you want to do is phase out the original staff and replace them with the people you want – most likely younger, cheaper and more pliable journalists. If you do too much of that the paper loses its character, but those considerations were swept aside and it was deemed that a younger cohort would "get" the requirements of the digital age faster and with more enthusiasm than the old guard.

In the shorter term you customise the system so that the newsroom has less control over its own working practices. In digital terms, this means analytics, and a small army of people in head office overseeing the metrics in operation in all their newsrooms. The digital team doesn't just measure how many clicks an article gets, it extracts lots more other data, including what time of day traffic peaks, where the readership is geographically located, what sort of stories are most read – and which journalists are getting the most clicks. This metric assumes that every click is equal, of course. It doesn't reflect on reader loyalty in the sense that it can't tell you if the online reader ever buys the print edition. It's just where do they click.

It's free to click, but that click matters a lot to the analytics team, and it certainly mattered to Trinity Mirror, who pretty soon started sending us ceaseless data about the number of viewers using the site on an almost hourly basis. OK – but a "top 10 clicks journalist"? This is a really tricky one. Such a metric is not a measure of talent, accuracy or quality. For instance, the crime reporter on a local newspaper is automatically going to get the most hits: that's just how it goes, and even if your crime reporter is a dullard – which the *News*' Raymond Brown certainly wasn't – he or she will get the hits regardless.

A chart of the top 10 most-read reporters on a week-by-week basis suggests someone somewhere doesn't appreciate human nature: this is a demeaning statistic to everyone, not just reporters. It elevates some reporters to the status of stars and what you really want as a journalist is to write stories because they are worthwhile and newsworthy, not necessarily because they will get clicks. The point is that the new praetorian guard of digital analysts "guide" the editor towards their preferred methodologies, and…. these analysts end up telling tell the editor what stories are and are not acceptable, telling him or her how long stories can and can't be and how many stories his or her reporters should be posting on a daily basis, with how many pictures and how many links to other stories.

In a previous era you'd respect an editor for his editorial judgement, the direction he took his paper in. It wasn't David Bartlett's fault that, under the Trinity Mirror playbook, all titles were expected to adhere to editorial policies that were set for the whole country, regardless of the strengths of individual titles. In Cambridge, for instance, Mike Richardson, when was managing director in the noughties, had said that "business in Cambridge is like the sports section of any other paper", meaning that the city followed what was being achieved in the same way as most towns follow their local football club – that is, with enthusiasm, faith, hope and gusto. But Trinity Mirror didn't see it that way. They wanted all their UK sites to have similar looking newspapers, and content that ticked their boxes. There would be no investment in the bizmag. Editorial content would be the same as everywhere else in the TM portfolio – lots of accidents, court cases, sport, crime and local council reports. Not so much business, thank you very much.

The steady trickle of people joining the *Cambridge Independent* continued late into 2016. The subject was an incessant topic of conversation: who was leaving, who might be next, what stories they were running. Any talk of disloyalty was by now a busted flush – the loyalty we had was for another organisation in the past, the Yattendon-owned *Cambridge News*, which had treated us with a semblance of dignity. You can't have loyalty to a new organisation, it's an oxymoron: loyalty takes time, and is not a given. By deliberately erasing its connection to the past, Trinity Mirror seemed to be signalling not only that it had no loyalty to the *Cambridge News*' past, but that it had no obligation of loyalty to its current staff either – and maybe not its future.

The loyalty question was totally parked up when it was discovered that Trinity Mirror had deleted the internet history of the *Cambridge News* from 2005 to 2015. All gone – everything we ever wrote. This was an act of potentially grievous harm to the careers of dozens of journalists. What happened to a journalist when they put on their CV, for instance, that they worked at the *Cambridge News* from 2007 to 2014? They wouldn't have kept the print versions of these stories: we'd gone digital, so you'd just post the link into the CV. But now you couldn't. The links were gone. Without those online records, you'd struggle to prove you even worked at the *Cambridge News* during that time.

It wouldn't have taken much to keep the archive on: just a flick of a digital switch. And in general, around a third of clicks on a newspaper website are for articles more than a week old, so they were cutting off a source of the very clicks they purported to be seeking. It was a shambles. Didn't they care enough about the journalists on the paper they had acquired to even try to get them on-side? The view in the newsroom was, at best, that this was an act of random vandalism, at worst an act of spite that was entirely unwarranted. It took years for Trinity Mirror, which changed its name to Reach in May 2018, to even install a search engine on its much-lauded new websites following the 2016 relaunch. Surely anyone knows a search engine is an integral part of a website? Apparently the news hadn't got to London. (A search facility for content from 2016 was installed a year after the relaunch.)

Bridges were not being repaired let alone being built, and the surviving edifices were under attack. An article in the *Press Gazette* in March 2017 summed up the situation. It reported the local MP, Daniel Zeichner, as saying that the loss of the *Cambridge News'* historic online content was a "real loss for Cambridge".

Zeichner said: "In the digital age we have all come to expect that the information will be available for us. The local newspaper is a key source of information for local people which is why they are so important."

An unnamed former senior editor of the *News* was then quoted in the *Press Gazette* as saying that the years of hard work that had gone into building the website was "a social history of Cambridge" that was now lost to the public.

He or she said: "For the last decade there must be thousands and thousands of articles on there and millions and millions of worlds which obviously together create a social history of Cambridge, of life in Cambridge and Cambridgeshire in the early 21st century.

"With the political stuff I would think there was some democratic duty to have that available. I think the politics and crime and those kinds of things should be there for people to see.

"The *Cambridge News* has been going since 1888. It's got a long history of being the paper of record for the city.

"Each newspaper owner has a right to pursue their own commercial strategy, but they are also the custodians of quite important democratic research and that comes with a certain amount of responsibility."

He or she added: "It makes me sad because we put so much time and effort into the website – especially because, like everybody, we were supposed to be pursuing a digital-first policy.

"All that time uploading millions of words to the website. It's an important resource and it seems crazy not to have it on there."

Trinity Mirror's position on the furore was quite clear: the website was now faster and had been redesigned to make it easier to read.

The going got tougher. More advertising reps were shown out of the building when it emerged that they were going to work "across the road". In a horrible ironic twist of the modern take on corporate etiquette, the bloke in charge of the laptop/mobile returns and escorted the reps off the premises was a few months later treated with similar disdain: he accepted redundancy after being made an offer that involved less pay, less status and more work, and off he went.

Sometimes the younger ad execs would tell me in confidence what they were doing before it was announced. They were clearly having a hard time of it. The future at the *News* looked bleak. Most of them were looking to get out, and it helped they were being offered more money to work across the road. It wasn't just the money, of course, that made it attractive: to sell – I knew this from my days as a salesman in the City in the 80s – you have to have some sort of belief, not just self-belief, but belief in what you're selling. Without that, your pitch is brain-dead, just one notch up from those cold calls you get on the phone when the voice says: "I hear you were involved in an accident and am here to help you make a claim". The *News* was on the way down just as the *Cambridge Independent* was starting up.

Respect may have been surplus to requirements at Trinity Mirror, but from the footfall in the second half of 2016 it wasn't out of fashion, and some of the older lads, like designer Jim Elsegood, made graceful exits. It was good to see Jim walk out with his head held high.

Meanwhile the young turks in the advertising department weren't hitting their targets. Previously there were print targets and digital targets, now they were added together and you had to hit both targets to get your bonus. Digital targets were sky-high and a lot of customers didn't want to be part of the website anyway, and it didn't help that the site was a ghastly mishmash of adverts and pop-ups which turned many off. Advertisers didn't appreciate being told they had to have a digital component to their order: cash is king, to lose sight of that is to ignore a key component of the economy. By insisting on a digital component to each sale, Trinity Mirror lost more print revenue than it needed to.

We did it slightly differently on the editorial side. When Andy Veale, the deputy editor who had become acting editor after Paul left, resigned, he worked his notice without comment and no comment was made about his decision by the riffraff (including me), either in the newsroom or outside in the shed where the smokers went for a break, or "a bit of fresh air" to use the preferred terminology. The fact that the editorial department was capable of being civilised about the change of the guard – no escorting people off the premises for our department – was one of the few good things during a troubled time.

Going off for a fag break meant a chance to have a natter free from the protocol of office codes. The regular shed-frequenters, who included non-smokers, were the indefatigable chief reporter Chris Elliott, who had been at the *News* for more than 30 years, Raymond Brown, Jenny, and the unflappable Russell Vaughan who was on the print hub and one of the most droll people you're ever likely to meet: his impersonations of familiar faces were and are hilarious.

We had our little bonding sessions outside the office too, of course, most notably in the pub. When Russell was laid off with the subs in 2011 we met up for a few beers, which inevitably became sessions where we would share the gossip of who was doing what to whom, along with all the trade talk, of power struggles and moves past, present and future on the chess board of our working lives. Those sessions were suspended three months after Russell was laid off: Paul Brackley, the editor at that time, had called him back in, and eventually he went back on a salary. His was one of the first instances of "over-sacking" in Cambridge, where so many people are laid off in one go the paper can't be produced properly, and those who were previously discarded are called up and asked to come in and do some shifts.

The Friday night sessions continued with uninterrupted enthusiasm, with the pub regulars becoming honorary comrades in arms in our struggle to promote the paper as part of the community, even as we were being sucked into the maw of a corporatocracy which was becoming increasingly unpleasant.

Mark Taylor, the chief sports reporter, was next to cross the road. His notice was served without comment from his comrades, and by Jenny and myself. Jenny and I had been attached to the sports desk over the years. After the first cull, of the subs, the staff count became so threadbare that two floors of our once-flashy Milton premises were no longer needed, and we all moved up to the top floor. Upstairs, we were mixed in with the advertising crowd, with distribution, design, subs, reporters, all crammed into one space. Downstairs was supposed to be let out but there were no takers: part of the reason may have been the woeful air conditioning/heating which we endured for years. One time the engineers came round to fix it and they started removing all the switches we'd been using to turn the heating or air conditioning up and down. I asked whether we would get replacements.

"No, mate," came the reply. "No need. These are all dummy switches anyway."

"Dummy switches," I stammered. "They don't work?"

"None of them would have made the slightest bit of difference, mate."

All those years of arguing among ourselves about whether the heating was too high or too low were a total waste of time: another example of our trusting natures!

Mark Taylor was sitting two seats down from me and Jenny while he served his notice. It was a good month, and he remained hugely productive, on time, always in a positive frame of mind, and no one ever mentioned the fact that he was going off to the other side. No one seemed to talk things through with Mark much though, or perhaps it was just me. I didn't make much effort, just one of those things. It was a balancing act sitting next to the sports team, because they had their chats about rugby or football or tennis and they didn't seem to much care for the opinions of outsiders and especially not casual fans like me. But I genuinely liked them and we had a fair few laughs over the years.

There was only one fall-out over all the time me and Jenny sat beside the sports hub. It was during the 2012 World Cup, and England were playing, the newsroom TV was on, it was ten feet from our desks, but the sound was off. I asked for the sound to be turned on and was told by the sports crew that the company "only had a licence for pictures", not sound, so the commentary for a live game had to be off. I launched into a rant about how likely it was that anyone from the licensing authority would turn up in reception demanding to see whether the TV sound was on or off, and whether we would all end up in jail if we were reported to the authorities for having the sound on, before just going for the jugular and accusing the sports guys of insane control freakery. Their stunned silence only gave me further licence to continue – England were playing rubbish football at the time, and I was actually outraged by the lack of gumption shown by the players on the pitch. Eventually someone went off to talk to someone in management and we were given "permission" to have the sound on. England lost anyway and were a complete shambles, of course.

If the manner of Mark's departure was creditable, so was that of his team mates. It was just sad, was all: people leaving a sinking ship. Fair play. Every person for themselves and all that.

The World Cup rant was pretty much my last. I'd had a few – drinks, battles, regrets, you name it – to my name and was in danger of becoming one of those office personalities Jenny called "a pastiche of themselves". That was pretty much her most scathing put-down, and I understood how it could happen. You get institutionalised, you're typecast, you play a part but Elvis left the building already. This not being a fate I wanted, I had to work out a way to avoid it, and I cast around for options.

While I was doing this, an incident kept coming to mind which I realised had a profound and long-lasting effect. It had occurred in 2006, when my much-loved aunt, Marjorie, was in her 90s and finding it hard to climb the stairs. She lived on her own in Hampton Court, and her financial affairs were controlled by a trust, a legacy of the old Bond family's wealth, which had helped her live in relatively pleasant circumstances along the banks of the river Thames. The trust was run by her nephew-in-law, David Richards. At the time, General Richards – now Lord Richards of Herstmonceux – was head of the British Army (Lord Richards was head of the armed forces from 2009 to 2013). He had married uncle Ken's daughter Caroline, by his first wife, Sue. So Caroline married David and David was in charge of the army's invasion strategies in Afghanistan and Iraq. He was also in charge of the trust which ran my aunt Marjorie's finances, and this trust was blocking Marjorie from having a stairlift.

At some point during a drawn-out and time-consuming negotiation I lost my rag and decided I would have to see this David Richards myself and ask him what he was playing at. Of course I couldn't discuss this with anyone in the family, because they would all have told me not to get involved, he could call in a helicopter squad and take us all down, but I was already in deep and I decided to track General Richards down.

This took a surprisingly long time: he'd served at Buckingham Palace, and getting details of his whereabouts proved harder than I imagined, but several weeks later I got his email, sent him a message, whereupon he invited me to his place of work to put my case. The place of work just happen to be the old War Office in Westminster, the very office from which Winston Churchill had run the campaigns of World War Two. I call it an office, but in fact it has 1,100 rooms.

I took the day off work for the visit, dressed smartly and made my way to the entrance, which was surrounded by police with Heckler & Koch machine guns cradled in their arms. This was well after the Iraq invasion, when the subsequent war was starting to prove uncomfortable. A new twist meant that terrorists were operating on the streets of European cities. Sadly, 52 people died in September 2005 when the London Underground system was targeted by Jihadis. By 2006, the time of this visit to the old War Office, the effort invested in Afghanistan was being ramped up and Camp Bastion was built in Helmand province in an attempt to conclusively defeat the Taliban. But the war had reached back home: the streets were no longer safe in the way that had been only a few years previously.

For weeks before the visit I pondered about whether to try saying something to General Richards about Afghanistan. Camp Bastion – now Shorabak – was on the road between Herat and Kandahar, the very road I'd travelled by bus in 1977, when a memorable incident had taken place...

When you leave Herat to go south-east you go along a road – the only sign of human life for hundreds of miles. Going through Helmand there are some incredible mountains, so bleak and imposing they look like moonrocks. You couldn't imagine anyone living there, so bare, no trees, a few bits of bracken, everywhere rock and dust. It was empty in a way I'd never conceived of before.

Out in that vast emptiness, the bus stopped by the side of the road for a break. Pretty much everyone got off to stretch their legs. Some passengers grabbed their baggage and started walking towards the mountains. I couldn't believe my eyes. There was nothing on that road, no shops, no petrol stations, nothing for 100 miles or more, not a single building, and no signs of any electricity pylons or other modern infrastructure. Just a narrow strip of tarmac and an invisible trail leading towards the mountains far away.

I watched these people walk off, and realised that your Afghani is a hardy soul: as tough as old boots, their resilience and tenacity were obvious. Watching them walk away, their spirits seemed indomitable. My respect for them soared to places I'd not known were available. These were warriors, each a prince among men. Their women were goddesses. Their eyes shone with the fervour of people in love with life at every moment. They bent the knee to no man and triumphed over whatever life threw at them.

Of those who remained some of the men – there were very few women travellers on roads in Afghanistan in 1977 – went round to the other side of the bus and began praying towards Mecca in the classic Muslim fashion, with their prayer mats spread over the sand. I stayed near by the bus door to be sure I didn't miss its departure. One of the Afghans sparked up a joint, and passed it round to a group of four or five chums. They all took one or two drags and passed it on, and one of them passed it to me. "Is very good!" I took it, had a couple of drags and passed it back. I'd heard about the strength and quality of Afghani Black hashish but I figured I should be able to handle a couple of puffs.

After passing it on, all seemed well for a minute or two, and pretty soon everyone clambered back on to the bus. As I started climbing the steps I felt a bit squiffy. When I got to the start of the rows of seats I fainted, just completely keeled over like a sack of potatoes, crumpled flat on my front and there I lay, as paralysed as if a black widow spider had administered a cocktail of inertia. And, in that strange state of mind, I heard the tinkling sound of laughter, and forced myself to look up.

Every single person on that bus was looking at me and laughing uproariously. The twinkles in their eyes would have fired up star systems. I felt a profound sense of gratitude and belonging. They could have just taken me down, thrown me out on the road, taken my stuff... no one would probably ever have found me. As I staggered to my seat I felt like the luckiest person alive, to have been treated so honourably by men who had probably fought off mountain lions and walked for five days through the desert without water to go home, using the stars as their map.

I kept thinking of these men prior to seeing David Richards, wondering whether I would get the chance to "have a word" with the army's chief strategist about messing with such people. If I got a chance, what would I say? "David, you will never defeat the Afghanis on their home territory. You will save a great number of lives, especially on our side, if you insist on a political solution to the problem rather than a military one, which can only have one outcome." Would I remind him of the first Anglo-Afghan war in the 19th century? Would I tell him about the Afghanis I had encountered on the bus to Kandahar, who knew every rock and shrub of Helmand, and explain to him that they could not be defeated?

I was taken to an ante-room in the Old War Office and watched the news on Sky TV on a wall-mounted screen alongside a bunch of officers and hangers-on for a few minutes, then was led into David's office. It was huge, vast, the size of a quarter of a football pitch. And there he was at his desk in the corner by a window, and he got up, shook my hand and took my coat which he hung on a coat stand. He invited me to sit down in the sofa area, and cups of tea were brought in. Pleasantries were exchanged.

"Now look," he said. "You know that as a trustee I am concerned about Marjorie, but the fact is that she could carry on living for another 20 years and we can't afford to empty the coffers on this stairlift, she's not had it so bad for all these years, I mean, she's done well, she's had lots of holidays out of this trust, and we just can't afford this sort of expense."

The "holidays" jibe was one I was prepared for. It was true that great-aunt Myrtle, who was Stanley Bond's wife, had wanted Marjorie to be looked after financially. Marjorie was the eldest of Charles Shaw Bond's children, and had helped her uncle Stanley in the 1920s when she was a young woman, making arrangements, booking hotels and tickets and generally helping organise his affairs. And Marjorie had never married, and great-aunt Myrtle had wanted her to be looked after properly. Myrtle was wealthy, and she set it out in plainspeak so every generation could understand what it was she wanted and expected from those who followed.

When David had finished, I put my teacup down on the saucer very slowly. There would be no rattling of teacups – let alone sabres – on this excursion.

"I understand perfectly what you are saying, David, but I have to remind you that the trust was specifically set up so that Marjorie should be able to live a full life and if, as part of that, she took some holidays in the 60s and 70s, then those were holidays she was perfectly entitled to take. No one can accuse her of living a hedonistic life now, even if you might think she did then. She is extremely frugal."

"As for knowing how long Marjorie has to live," I continued, "none of us knows that for certain, but I see her every weekend and she is now very frail. She is in good spirits, but without a stairlift she's sleeping on her sofa, and is unable to have a bath, and that is not a suitable arrangement for someone who we all love very dearly."

"I understand that," said David, "but it would be irresponsible of me to dip into the reserves to pay for a major renovation like this at this time. Perhaps it can be arranged for more carers to assist her."

The Afghans on the bus seemed to be huddled together in a corner of the room, watching me, counting time. I was just a curiosity to them. Their arms were folded, they expected nothing from the situation. I was just another Westerner who had failed them. A huge sadness overwhelmed me. I had let them down, and now I was going to fail my dear aunt Marjorie too. I cast about for some way out, but there was none. I looked at David, a man who evaluated the lives and deaths of men as part of his remit. He'd made his mind up, probably well before I'd even walked through the door. I was massively irritated by his attitude, and I had two options: I could argue, or I could thank him and leave. Option one would serve no purpose other than to mildly annoy him, and that could have negative consequences, some of which could impact on aunt Marjorie, and that would be counterproductive.

"OK," I said. "I'm sorry to hear the trust can't finance the stairlift, but it was good of you to see me and I appreciate your time." I established that he would contact me as and when, wished his family well, and got up to leave.

It was at this point that David did something that stayed with me, which I remembered years later when I was trying to devise a survival strategy for the battles coming down the line in the newsroom. He got up and walked over to the coat stand, took down my coat and held it open so that I could comfortably fit into it without struggling to put it on myself. He did it exactly as a hotel concierge or doorman would do, and waited patiently while I faffed about trying to get my arms to go in the right place. That was impressive etiquette: a powerful man, who has just had an encounter with a chippy member of his wife's family, still remembered his manners as his guest was leaving. It was a hugely considerate gesture and softened me towards him, and by the way it also helped that the stairlift was installed two months later. But what stayed with me was David's exquisite manners. If I could develop and refine etiquette to that level, might that not be of some use as the world we knew was thrown to the lions?

So I settled on becoming the inverse of the mouthy gob I was in danger of becoming. I would become someone who was courteous. It was, in fact, the only stone in the office canon that I hadn't turned over. I couldn't save the Afghanis on the bus, though.

– Chapter 29 –

Being polite was a good option for negotiating the newsroom, and it became even more of a necessity in the context of the significant shift in British history that took place on June 23rd, 2016 – the day the EU Referendum was held.

It felt like an odd referendum to be holding. There was no particular need for a vote, but the governing Conservative party felt that one was necessary to clear up "once and for all" the long-time anti-European stance which some members of their party were advocating. The prime minister had offered to hold the referendum during the 2015 election campaign, to head off apparently significant number of Conservative voters who were considering backing the right-wing UK Independence Party (UKIP), although UKIP didn't actually have any Members of Parliament.

The outcome was driven by a large number of older Brits who wanted out of the EU. I found it odd that an older generation hankered after a past they surely knew was pretty awful in certain key respects. The power cuts that happened in the 1970s, when the electricity firms went on strike, were symptomatic of a troubled country that had been labelled "the sick man of Europe". Losing that tag had taken three decades. A great deal of progress had been made in terms of expanding horizons and embracing the wider world. But, for some, this progress was a source of resentment, and they wanted someone to blame for the austerity years too. When presented with a chance to blame the EU, they took it.

Internationalism was a good thing for someone like me, the son of a first generation immigrant with one French grandmother and one Italian grandfather. Both of my father's parents were Jewish, and the images of Jews being herded on to trains 60 years before, heading east, once understood, was never going to go away. No matter I'm not Jewish, anyone with the family surname I bore would be on the list to go east if such a list was to be drawn up again. You can't erase knowing that. A united Europe meant there was less chance of that happening.

A couple of weeks before the EU referendum Charlie was at home, visiting from Madrid where he was making a living teaching English to students and office workers. He was mildly optimistic.

"Hopefully it'll be okay," he said when we talked about it in the kitchen at the family home. "I imagine it'll be 60/40 in favour of staying."

I hoped he was right. Charlie wasn't the only one of our three children living on the European mainland: Flo's home was Vlaardingen, near Rotterdam, in the Netherlands, where she'd been living for five years with her partner Thijs, a captain in a shipping firm. Leaving the EU would directly impact her, because she worked for a UK-based charity and was paid in sterling, and the value of the pound would be impacted. Flo's brother, too, would have to watch what happened to the rights of EU nationals living in Britain and British nationals living in the EU.

The campaign to stay in the EU was lukewarm: you too often got the feeling from politicians at the time that either their hearts weren't in it or they didn't really know what the advantages of staying in the EU were. Perhaps they thought it was obvious, but they didn't connect with the populace too well. I guess it's hard to advocate not doing something. Along with millions of others I was horrified at the way it went.

One of the awful consequences of the outcome of the vote was that social media platforms were full of the most horrendous vitriol. People who were apparently friends turned on each other in the most personal ways and, in the aftermath, many friendships would be broken, and family members would become estranged from each other in the same way as had occurred during the miners strike in the mid-1980s. Social media wasn't quite the same after the summer of 2016: people understood that the thin soil it provided was home to a savage bear pit, as far from the global village utopia as you could imagine.

From being a benign way of having a conversation with friends, family and colleagues, Facebook and Twitter quickly became a massive bitch-fest and Brexit amplified and encouraged the mayhem. However, as is now being more full understood, Facebook's business model makes money from impulses which are broadly narcissistic in nature, so it was only a question of time. What else could you expect? It's inevitable that subtlety, shade, indifference and neutrality would be drowned out in the cacophony of attention-seeking.

This drowning-out was also encouraged by media owners whose newspapers shrieked jingoistic sentiments. Apparently it mattered not one jot to readers that these men – Murdoch at News International, the Barclay brothers at the *Telegraph*, the Rothermeres who owned the *Daily Mail*, and Richard Desmond at the *Daily Express* – often lived overseas and conducted their financial affairs from offshore tax havens. They put their own interests first, and aggressively campaigned to promote those interests through their newspapers. The tragedy of Britain's post-referendum position has been that the readerships of these right-wing papers failed to understand the contempt in which their owners held them, and failed to see that their motive was to get the political classes to back policies – essentially the US model of low taxes and minimal state interference – which would be very bad news for the National Health Service and welfare budgets. These owners thought about one thing only: it was all about how they could make more money. And they played people who fretted about their supposedly diminished status in the world.

It didn't help that the BBC seemed to freeze up over Brexit. The coverage was benign about the disinformation and half-truths. Pro-Brexit politicians were given an easy ride, those wishing to stay in the EU were challenged and derided. But if significant sections of the national media acted as cheerleaders-in-chief for Brexit and stirred dormant xenophobic fantasies, there were honourable exceptions, including the *Guardian* and the *Independent*. They were up against the *Telegraph, Times, The Sun* and *Mail,* each of which formatted their news output to suit the agendas of their owners and used the journalists on their books to perpetuate the illusion that Brexit would usher in a fabulous new dawn for Britain. If a journalist on one of these titles wanted to keep their job, they toed the line. Telling people when they're being hoodwinked is part of journalism's remit, but the alarm bells were not rung.

All journalism has been diminished by this. Press ownership is a contentious subject but the key point is that a journalist be able to express his or her views freely and accurately, within the law. The weight of responsibility to be able to write with" neither fear nor favour" allows journalism to hold those in power accountable to the people and communities they serve. It is effectively a branch of democracy. But this transparency was missing in action over Brexit. No one told the British public that you can't have your cake and eat it. Politicians lied about the consequences, and reporters fed junk promises into a machine that encouraged and fooled Britons into making scapegoats of those least responsible for the financial crisis. This was a dereliction of duty by the journalistic cadre which has had huge consequences for the way the media is perceived on both sides of the Atlantic.

The Brexit vote was just the start of it. The run-in to the US election in November 2016 had a huge impact on journalism. The term "fake news" was coined during this campaign. Technology meant that any sort of tittle-tattle could be half-way round the world before the truth got its britches on. The ease of clicking on a link – no upfront financial investment required – meant that junk news would always be given an equal hearing with a news report, and fact-checkers would always be playing catch-up.

But even if the term was deployed on an industrial scale after 2016, the dynamics of fake news were not new. Some, like Yuval Noah Harari, say that fake news started with the Bible. The stories about some events, perhaps such those involving the Babylonian king Nebuchadnezzar, Harari says are backed up by the evidence of literature and excavations. Others, such as the story of the creation of the Garden of Eden, are just fake news, though some might say that he's over-dignifying the proposition by adding the word "news" at all.

In more modern times, the coffee houses that sprang up in the 17th century were the Facebook platforms of their day. When political dissent became too intense in 1672, Charles II issued a proclamation "to restrain the spreading of false news". In 1924, the *Daily Mail* published the forged Zinoview Letter four days before a general election: the letter was a fake directive from Moscow to British communists to activate "sympathetic forces", and the Labour Party lost the election in a landslide. The British government led the Germans to believe the 1944 Normandy landings would take place elsewhere. The assassination of John F Kennedy in 1963 was implausibly sold as the work of a lone lunatic rather than the work of a group or even organisations: very possibly this is a chapter of fake news yet to be fully unravelled. And, as we have seen, the death of 96 people at Hillsborough in 1989 was followed by a fake news campaign which involved the police and the *Sun* newspaper.

This century, the "weapons of mass destruction" charge against Saddam Hussein's Iraq in the run-up to the Iraq War was complete fakery. The journalists who reported it were recording fake news – they didn't know it, but some suspected it for sure. There are even those who suggest that 9/11 itself was a giant fake news program – but right now that suggestion is a conspiracy theory. In some ways, fake news and conspiracy theories are similar – both act as propaganda for whoever is creating them, and anti-propaganda for other theories (which may have a better connection to the truth).

What we can say about fake news is that it is the deliberate broadcasting of falsehoods by individuals working in the media or in media-related fields who know what they are saying or writing is untrue, but go ahead and put it out anyway. The scale and typology of this behaviour, the number of people such falsehoods can reach and the condensed timeframes involved – which allow the worldwide broadcasting of such content within seconds and make it hard to refute before it gains traction – is entirely new, which is why a new phrase has been coined for it.

Some of those broadcasting fake news work for, or represent, governments and corporations – the Russian state's involvement in the generation and broadcasting of fake news has reached epidemic proportions – but some work for newspapers. Of those who work for newspapers, some are knowingly paid by their owners to muddy the waters of public discourse. The outcome is that the covenant between the media and the public has been weakened – to deliberately unravel the bond is the intention of unscrupulous press barons and corporate interests. This process has accelerated in the last two decades, and that is a new phenomenon. In time, the public has inevitably become suspicious of all news, and this suspicion became outright distrust – and indeed loathing – just in time for the 2016 American presidential election, which gave the non-politician Donald Trump the keys to the White House.

American journalists in particular were caught on the hop with Trump's penchant for tweeting in the early hours. It messed with the news cycle. It didn't help that the need for accuracy which had been sacrosanct to a previous generation of reporters had been eroded by the sheer volume of stories journalists were expected to produce. It meant that journalists just repeated what others said had happened, what someone else said, or what people were saying about it on Facebook or Twitter, because they didn't have time to consider how much of it was true or not – or fact-check it.

As journalists came under pressure to deliver more stories in less time, it became possible to quasi-invent a story, so a reporter could call someone and say "I've heard so-and-so is a tax dodger, can you comment please?" Then you take the comment back to the person involved and they react to the comment with a denial, which will probably leave some questions unanswered. The gaps might be relevant, or they might not be. Either way… Bingo: instant story. Artificial, but readable. Better than a fake news story, but you've lost the ethical high ground. And from there the slope only gets slipperier, which is great if your interest is in propaganda rather than truth.

Putting "real" news side by side with fake news skews the logic of the business model. Might it not be more expedient to just run, if not fake news, then stories that are perhaps badly researched, badly written, but click-bait friendly? After all, the readers are so fickle, so demanding, they just want more stories, and research is actually a hindrance because no one wants to read a 2,000-word article any more – says this logic, broadcast by propagandists for the corporates. What they are saying is this: 'People are too stupid to understand complex arguments any more. We know they're stupid because we've run the education system into the ground.'

If two stories are put together online, and one says "Rhinos face extinction as illegal traffic in horns soars", and the other says "Why the Queen is a lesbian", then which story will people click on? That's right – your guess is as good as mine. It depends a lot on culture and education but human nature, as we are now discovering, often makes choices based around getting a quick dopamine fix to the brain rather than anything resembling analytical thinking.

In another age, most people believed in a god, but we are not in a formally religious age, religions now being associated with fanaticism of one variety of another, so false gods are lined up to take advantage of the gap in supply. And on the back of the economic benefits of our nascent new world order something else is being piggy-backed in: an ability to tinker with the very blueprint that humanity has been subject to thus far. That's the part that was being plugged into by earlier generations: now we can have a mini-Godlike experience on social media platforms on a regular basis, it's getting harder for organised religions to compete. It's partly supply-and-demand economics, but it's also basic wiring: people are hardwired to connect with their immediate environment first. If there is a a bit of time left over, then it's okay to dabble in the arts, or religion, but survival is the motivation, danger is the measure of its success. Being in on the loop of information means being forewarned of possible danger, and gossip is its early warning system. Access to gossip has evolutionary advantages. Knowing where to find cheap bread or good medicine helps. So does knowing if someone is a thief, or a serial seducer. If the information can help protect or feed you and your family this week, it will be of more use than warnings about some hell – including climate change events that may or may not happen – further down the line. Such warnings can be set aside in the hardball of daily life.

A journalist is, or should be, an outsider: he or she has to have contact with the leaders in its community, but they are not or should not be answerable to them. The high point of US journalism was Watergate, the break-in scandal which had toppled President Richard Nixon in the early 1970s. The journalists at the *Washington Post*, Carl Bernstein and Bob Woodward, displayed courage, tenacity and intelligence in the way they unpicked events. It was two years from the break-in at the Democratic Party's Watergate office to the resignation of the president. Could you imagine two journalists being allowed to follow a story for two years now? Two weeks is pushing it, though there are honourable exceptions including the Panama Papers reporting, the research on the Facebook/Cambridge Analytica scandal, and the Windrush deportation crisis.

Journalism's low point was surely around the time of the US-led invasion of Iraq in 2003: the media adopted a supine, no-questions-asked approach which green-lighted disaster. It was just: "Saddam Hussein was responsible for 9/11? Let's get him!" American troops were fed into a failing state's death spiral and the media urged it all on. To even dare to pose a question about whether the invasion of a sovereign state, which had no terrorist infrastructure, was a legitimate course of action was not a question too many US journalists seemed willing to ask. The elephant in the room, post 9/11, was the role of Saudi Arabia in the attack on the Twin Towers, but America was at that point entirely beholden to its addiction to oil and any participation by Saudis was played down, while the rhetoric and the consequences of war were deliberately misdirected to another country which was punished in its stead.

People aren't stupid. As battle was waged with massive civilian casualties in appalling acts across the globe, everyone had to work out for themselves whether something was going horribly wrong or not. Writers are answerable to readers, the people who buy their paper, who invest their time and money in the product. Their purchase buys a right to accurate information, but the information trail had been diluted over the years, the poached became the gamekeepers, and the information machine became more one-dimensional. A previous generation of journalists would have had time to discuss how to respond to events. This was now out of the question due to time and money restrictions. The public sensed the media had played a role in the manipulation of the American people and they concluded that the media – perhaps more than the elites who had acquired the levers of power – couldn't be trusted. After all, you sort of know that elites can't be trusted… It was on the back of this whole sordid debacle that Donald Trump came to power.

Trump used Twitter to bypass the media and talk directly to the American people, and they loved it. The role of the media as the interface between those in power and the voters who put them there was fractured. Part of the reason was the internet, part of it was a dereliction of duty by way of incapacitation. The industry was rightly given a hard time, but the wrong perpetrators were in the public's dock.

The function of news was no longer restricted by truth-telling, it was all about spectacle, and journalists were in danger of becoming part of a circus act of fame and distraction, at the same time being more reluctant to step out of line in an environment in which they were being culled mercilessly. And those journalists who would conventionally have sounded the alarm were being made mute by the arrival of the internet, and by the populist insurgency that Trump headed in the US and Brexiteers – whose campaign was given unequivocal support by many media barons – in the UK. By mute, read redundant.

It was carte blanche for a story to be declared "fake news" if it contained anything someone didn't want the public to know. The whole atmosphere around politics and cultural life become very tangled. All you had to do was add the internet and you'd never be able to go someplace where the fireball wouldn't reach you.

– Chapter 30 –

If Trinity Mirror's antics were driven by a desire to reboot the newsroom into a digitally-led machine, geared to clicks, browsers and audience traffic, the *Cambridge Independent* seemed to be taking a different tack.

The *Cambridge Independent* offering did include a website, of course, but not all the content was posted online. The idea seemed to be for people to buy the print version first: the digital component was not a replacement for the print edition, but a shout-out for it. To start with this seemed unforgivably retro, but gradually the sheer logic of the situation re-rendered it as rather astute. The digital readership had no loyalty to the paper or its journalists, so why spoon-feed one market free content and expect another to pay for it? The digital edition, as those left at the *Cambridge News* began to realise, was undermining the print edition, even though the print edition was what was bringing the revenue in. This made no business sense.

The idea that digital revenue would one day overtake print revenue was as far off as ever. Trinity Mirror's plan was to have equal digital and print revenues – 50/50 – within two years, but that would only be achieved by winding down print revenue, undermining the print edition to the point that it was no longer worth buying. The suggestion that growing digital revenue to the point that it was the dominant part of the equation was years away for regional newspapers. Even if the plan eventually yielded the revenue streams required to sustain the infrastructure of newspaper production, it would be too late for journalism to continue to fulfil its central role of holding the institutions of power to account.

Newsrooms were in danger of becoming an instrument of the powerful, accountable only to owners, no longer independent – just a branch of public relations. If you own a newspaper, and you have business dealings with China, for instance, you might decide that kow-towing to Beijing should include avoiding any mention of Tibet in your papers. If you're a Russian oligarch, and you own a paper in the UK, you might want to be careful about how your paper reports on Vladimir Putin's antics. And so it goes.

I was still in the maw of the realisation that manners maketh man. Every situation highlighted the role that etiquette plays in our lives. It also became clear that the use of etiquette could be deployed to mask a person's inner state. Someone new to the newsroom, for instance, could use etiquette as a shield, to avoid difficult situations. That is understandable: walking into an unfamiliar workplace can be a formidable experience and certainly it had taken me years to get to know my comrades, but the new generation didn't have years and they had careers to fast-track.

It struck me how little people were caring about their own wellbeing as the workplace changed, and how little mental and emotional health was valued by their employers, not just in the media, but every workplace which involves sitting in front of a computer for long hours. We're the first generation to have experienced these conditions: are we really building a better society as a result of the sacrifices we make? Who knows what illnesses or woes we may be storing up for the future?

In late 2016 another change was introduced: "shared content". This involved some pages being created at Trinity Mirror's Liverpool site and being made available to its dozens of sites across the country. The puzzle pages, for instance, didn't need to be produced locally. They were created in Liverpool. Then came film, book and TV reviews. At what point would the local paper cease to be local? Liverpool also had a department producing motoring stories and road tests: I still laid them out on the page, and I could use local stories, but using Liverpool as a resource for stories meant a loss of autonomy. I didn't test drive so many cars any more, but the day it became clear that local road tests were now surplus to requirements was still dispiriting.

A car maker would release a new model and they organised a review for motoring teams by sector. You would get invited to visit Ford in Dagenham to road-test their new ranges. By now there were fewer motoring journalists and there was no need to have a significant press fleet for use by the media. Many of these press fleets and the expensive press trip new car launches were disbanded. It wasn't good for us because our advertising revenue came from local dealerships, and they liked having a road test involving a car that was photographed in a local setting by a recognisable writer who had a voice in the community. Now all that was gone, or going.

Commercial features and even national news pages were being produced up north and then distributed to Trinity Mirror's sites via wire as single images for use in the newspaper. These images – .jpgs in technical speak – couldn't easily be altered even if there was a mistake.

Other parts of the production process were taken out of our hands. The story count – the number of stories on a page – was decreasing. On an average page there had been eight stories – the lead, a picture story, some down page stories, a bunch of short news stories called nibs (news in brief)... over a period of three years this story count was cut to a lead and a picture story. Same cover price, but a lot cheaper to produce.

Some of the weekly newspapers' offices were shut: where there had been eight, there was now just Ely, Newmarket and Royston. Eventually these would go too. The number of people no longer in the workplace made it feel empty: what had happened to the typographers and print specialists years before had cascaded down to the copy runners, the copy inputters, van delivery drivers, librarians, receptionists, subs, ad reps... it was ongoing.

Three years earlier the then deputy editor, Paul Kirkley, a huge talent, had joked in print about following the machinations' logic to its conclusion, and he'd written eventually you'd find a man in a darkened room hunched over a spreadsheet calculating the PnL – the profit and loss – of a million clickbait stories published using an AI-generated news algorithm. That was a bit prescient, in retrospect: the notion of stories generated by algorithms was given legs in 2017 when the Press Association, PA, said it was going to generate stories gathered – "harvested" in business-speak – from official sites including the council, the police, ambulance and fire services. They would then be slightly rewritten from various angles for various corporate customers, all by machine...

But people weren't just being laid off: some left to go and work elsewhere, even in other industries. The head of sport went to head up a charity's communication department. One news editor went to a medical firm's communications team, another joined the university's comms team. Jonathan Tewson went to Newmarket Racecourse. Nigel Brookes, the man who had given me my job 20 years earlier, retired: he had really been put through the mangle over the years, and ended up as editor of the weekly titles only to see the ground beneath his feet hacked away as the weeklies were gradually closed. After a few weeks, he came back as a temporary production sub, declaring he was much happier with his new status, and indeed he looked ten years younger. Others went to work for pharma companies, or PR firms, or the council. The ties of the old life were not broken easily, but they were being steadily dismantled.

Early in 2017 a new round of redundancies was announced in yet another company meeting in the conference room: it included the office manager, the very wonderful Roz Lau, two photographers and two designers – who was to go was to be decided in a consultation round – and the "business sub-editor". That meant me, though no one was named in that meeting.

"Business sub-editor" was an imaginary job – my job title was "Business writer, motoring editor and commercial features content manager" – but I knew the game was up because the evening before I'd been sent an email asking me to go and see the editor first thing in the morning, and straight away I'd gone outside with Jenny and told her the news, with strict instructions that this time she was not to get involved. She accepted – it was a sombre moment – and said she hoped my reading of the situation was wrong.

The early-morning meeting involved the editor, David Bartlett, and an HR person, Emma. They both looked extremely smart. David read out a prepared Trinity Mirror script and asked me if I had any questions. I said I didn't have any questions but I wanted him to know that he could be completely confident about my professionalism throughout the process. He said I would be asked to attend another meeting later in the week to discuss the details.

It was hard to know what to think but one thing was clear: I had made a miscalculation in that I had convinced myself that because I was able to both write and do page production – a feat few co-workers could match – I would be deemed too useful to replace. I was actually holding down roles in commercial features, motoring and business, with daily dialogues with reporters, designers, the advertising department, photographers… the whole show. But no one was irreplaceable and in fact it was precisely this multitasking that was no longer required. Trinity Mirror wanted one person to do one job. That way the metrics for that person's production could be more effectively tracked. Interdepartmental skills and roles were messy and were not part of the new vision for the newsroom. The complexity of tasks in my job description wasn't trackable, and I was out.

– Chapter 31 –

When you work for a large organisation there are various functions the company performs on your behalf and, over time, you take these functions for granted.

If you stay for more than, say, ten years, your social life will probably involve your work colleagues, even your romantic world, and the routine of your working week is central to your life until the company resembles the mothership and all the other things you do are secondary to the primary function of your existence, which is to be on the mothership, at your desk, doing the job which justifies your existence. And now, thanks to technology, there's the additional expectation that even if you are not at your desk, you'll still be available at all times of the day.

There is progress, of course. A couple of years before I left the *News* I got kitted out with a beautiful new Dell laptop which meant I could do almost all my work at home. Whereas before if there was a problem with one of my pages – it would happen every few weeks – I would have to get in the car late at night, drive to the office, fire my computer up and sort the issue out so the press could resume printing. Now I could just open my laptop and resend the page from home. That certainly felt like progress.

But the working week is such that a weekend is a brief chance to catch up on some sleep and wave at your family and friends. A holiday allows you to only partially recharge your physical, emotional and mental batteries before you go back to the fray, and if you're able to book a two-week holiday you will actually miss your work after ten days. Not in a dreamy way, but viscerally. All journalists thrive on adrenalin, but you will also miss the fact that you sit at your desk complaining about all the aspects of life you're missing while you're sitting there.

There is an element of being institutionalised in any organisation, but I didn't bother about it too much, because I'd weathered the possibility of being institutionalised at boarding school and knew the pitfalls and how to avoid them, plus I'd fully charged the "life" component of my work-life balance during my India and Glastonbury years. But I could see it happening around me. One of the sports guys was looking forward to retiring for years. He'd go on and on about it, and it was years away. He made it sound like real life, the world outside the *News*, like land is to a sailor who's been at sea for several years. For the most part I didn't know whether to laugh or cry. "Life's this minute and I'm in it!", Jenny used to say, and I concur.

Working for a corporation involves teamwork, and there are benefits to being a team player: Yuval Noah Harari, in his magnificent "Sapiens: A Brief History of Humankind", points out that without cooperation on a mass scale humankind would not be the dominant species on this planet.

In a newsroom you're part of a team, or several teams in my case, and being a journalist is a highly creative and skilled job. Hopefully the cogs all mesh together and this amazing achievement can be enjoyed by millions, though even a few thousand will do. If you set yourself personal goals and challenge yourself along the way you'll be happier and more fulfilled. You have to surprise yourself, so you might look back at something you've written way back and think yes, that's stood the test of time, that was adding to the store of human knowledge in some small or obscure way.

People have been using smartphones and laptops for a tiny amount of time in terms of the shift from the Industrial Age to the Technology Age. Incredibly quickly, we have integrated a dizzying array of gadgets into our lives, and sometimes you wonder: what would life be without it? Would I even be able to survive without all this stuff?

I had no idea what the future held but, in early 2017, my first task was to negotiate my way out of the Trinity Mirror hall of mirrors with as much dignity as was manageable in the circumstances. That meant not leaving with our tails between our legs.

After the formal meeting with HR came another meeting with the editor and a member of the editorial team. At this meeting I stated my intention of making the process as straightforward as possible, and added that I would be working in the city as a freelancer and considered it entirely possible that the *Cambridge News* would become a client.

This meeting went well, but on a subsequent occasion David was discussing future arrangements on the business desk when he mentioned that there were "other possibilities". This was the moment Jenny had schooled me to listen out for. When that happens, she said, "don't close the door. Listen to what he has to say." I'd talked myself through various ways this moment might arrive and what I'd do when it did. At all costs, I said to myself, keep the dialogue open. Listen to what he has to say.

"How do you mean?" I asked when the moment came.

"Well, there could be a role on the production team," David said.

At that moment all my schooling went out of the window, and I just tutted. It was an entirely involuntary reaction. After tutting, embarrassed by the lack of professionalism and courtesy that such a response suggested and, as much to cover up the bad taste of my rejoinder as anything else, I added: "I don't think that would be suitable for me at this point. The production hub is looking pretty full up anyway."

David didn't elaborate on exactly what the offer entailed. I'd already rejected it. The outcome was that I wasn't going to work on the production hub but I was going to take the redundancy option in a very professional manner.

Maybe I shouldn't have tutted but I had to forgive myself because it was involuntary, it was my body's reaction to a distressing idea. Fact was, working on the production hub – what had been the subs desk 20 years before – had been hardwired into my body. My body said it wasn't going back there and that was that. Quite right too. The difficulties of being at your desk all day, every day, were not offset by interviewing amazing people, or going out to magical launches and events. There would be no emails announcing scientific advances that would render you speechless, no phone calls to world-class scientists and business leaders… the production hub felt like a form of purgatory. Yes the business side was incredibly hard work, but it was all in pursuit of advances being made by the people in Cambridge's scientific and technology hub. It felt worthwhile. The advances were beneficial to humanity's ability to withstand disease or alleviate poverty. But so what: twenty years of hard work were now being scaled back to zero in the month it took to work my notice.

Leaving a place of work is a drag, even if you've only been there a few months. It's a drag for you and a drag for everyone else, some of whom are thinking: "What, are you still here, I thought you said you were off, so it's business as usual is it – all talk no walk?" Of course they are far too polite to say so, but if it does happen you have to find something humorous and on point to say in response. What you don't want is pity.

Even before a departure date was given, I was scouting around for what to do next. There are two options when you're trying to work out a major life decision: one is to aim for the moon, and the other is to keep buggering on, and I pursued both.

On the moonshot I'd already coined a phrase a couple of years previously, when I'd applied for a role as joint head of a local NGO hub, the Humanitarian Centre. The slogan was "I want to work for the community, not for the man." Flo had worked for this Cambridge organisation for 18 months, between university and going to live in the Netherlands, and the work they were doing was really encouraging, especially in Africa.

The Humanitarian Centre (now the Centre for Global Equality) supports were some amazing charities, like Street Child World Cup, which hosts a football tournament for street children every four years in the country where the World Cup proper is held. And individuals like Ken Banks, who had won a National Geographic Young Explorer award and adapted mobile telephony for use in farming and health collectives in Africa, really had a positive footprint, so when I saw the job I'd asked for my friend William, who I'd originally met in the 1970s at Northwick Park Hospital, if he'd jobshare it with me and he agreed to start an application process. William knew how to run a charity, as I well knew from years of being a trustee to the organisations he served. And just from the longevity perspective alone, this was a remarkable friendship which had endured through thick and thin. What is it they say? "You can't make new old friends."

The Humanitarian Centre application came to nought but what emerged from the process was that it was a good idea to dedicate some time to projects of personal interest. My personal interest being in charities and NGOs, I'd resolved to keep an eye open for those who were working and thinking creatively to develop practical solutions for all sorts of global problems and issues.

One of the NGOs at the Humanitarian Centre was Hoveraid, and while working my notice I saw a tweet in which they advertised for a photo-journalist for their aid work in Madagascar, where they deliver food and medicine by hovercraft to otherwise-inaccessible people in the north of the island. That was one strand to aim for: my moonshot.

The other plan, "keep buggering on", acquired wheels when the third member of the business desk, Matthew, who had joined a couple of years previously and was by now hugely proficient at his role, forwarded me an email from someone he knew in the property sector. The email asked if Matthew knew of anyone who was looking for part-time work. I thanked Matthew and arranged to have coffee with the founder of the firm in question in late February – another Matthew – three weeks before my departure date.

I liked the property idea, which was basically replicating a successful property platform based in London for Cambridge. I agreed to help set up shop for Matthew after leaving the *News*. This involved producing stories for this new property title. He mentioned that the firm's technology was all Mac-based, and it would be easier to set up if I had a Mac. So, with the assistance of the ever-wonderful Maria, a Spanish colleague working in Cambridge's marketing sector whose comradeship was also an amazing source of inspiration, I bought a MacBook Air with a top-spec helpline service. Finally, I commissioned a website for my new vehicle, Cambridge Open Media, and changed my Twitter handle to *@CambsOpenMedia*. I had 1,000-odd followers who I'd worked hard to amuse and inform, and porting them into the new name proved straightforward, which was a relief.

The practical details of leaving a journalistic post include selecting your best work and saving it to a memory stick or posting it to your personal email. This was complicated by that fact that the *Cambridge News*' archive had been deleted some months earlier. I asked an old chum, Bernard Adams, if there was any way of tracking down the back catalogue. Bernard had started a very successful motorcycle training firm, CamRider, some years previously, as part of a Prince's Trust scheme. It became a popular franchise and a model for motorcycle training in the UK. Bernard always had the best – and the coolest – people working for him, and they clearly respected and loved their boss and their jobs. After sitting with Bernard for an hour he worked out how to get to find a lot of the *Cambridge News* links, about a third of the archive, via an old server which could be somehow temporarily reactivated, but each link took so long to hunt down and load that it wasn't practical. Our backstory really had been eliminated.

I was lucky because the bizmag was online as an e-reader, so I could download the pdfs of the page and use them as a record. The only other way to record any work was to keep the print editions, but since Lorraine had left some years previously there was no complete print record of everything that was produced. We'd snookered ourselves, or at least been snookered.

The countdown proceeded with various handovers and discussions on how the work I'd been doing would be taken on by other departments and individuals. A freelance content manager, Stephen, would take on the motoring. He came over to ask about how it all worked. That was emotional: I'd been motoring editor for 15 years, and it took 20 minutes to hand it over to Stephen, one of the production team. Some of that time I was close to tears but I don't think he noticed because after 20 years in the newsroom I'd become more competent at censoring what my face wanted to project, especially when in difficulties.

It gave me no satisfaction that there would be no more motoring editors, just a variety of content managers minding shop. The motoring heyday had been a decade and more before, but I still nurtured it like you would a sick puppy, hoping against hope that a way might be found to revive it, even as the industry was changing, not just from online but also because of the arrival of hybrid drivetrains and all-electric car options, both of which had fewer moving parts, meaning that the vast industry of mechanics, parts and servicing would be gradually wound down in the same way as my own industry seemed to be being wound down. I choked up as I was talking through the production process with Stephen because even if I was handing over a busted flush it was still somehow my bambino and then suddenly it wasn't, and I was surprised at how deep those feelings went.

The clock wound down and the two options for a post-*News* career presented themselves. One was to go to Madagascar for six months to work with Hoveraid, the other was to take on the property role. I couldn't say no to the property role, as that was paid, so that was a cert, and I kept talking to Hoveraid. The issue with going away for six months was that the house would have to be rented out, as the charity was only paying expenses. I discovered from the discussions I had with a former Hoveraid worker that there was some flexibility in the starting date, so I resolved to have the house ready for renting out by the start of May, which gave me six weeks to sort it out.

The next few weeks would prove incredibly challenging, and obliged me to reconsider all my assumptions about wellbeing, mental health and the purpose of economic activity. The cans that had been kicked down the road were all there, waiting to be picked up. And now I had the time to do that: there were no more excuses.

– Chapter 32 –

The first thing you lose when you quit work is your status. Just a few months before I could have emailed or contacted Cambridge's most eminent businessmen and women, and arranged to discuss their projects and ambitions. Now, I was like a discarded sandwich wrapper. Outside the corporate structure that cocooned me in its world, who was I?

I wore myself down. I'd never had sleeping problems before, and suddenly, if I did manage a couple of hours' kip I'd wake an hour before dawn, eyes wide open, a feeling in my gut like a horse just kicked me, adrenalin coursing through me like a rutting stag, turning to panic and resulting in anxiety attacks which got so bad I worried about having a heart attack.

During the day I was working to get the house ready to rent out so I could go to Madagascar. This involved a lot of sorting out – of books, papers, old clothes, stuff going way back. I hadn't done a major clear-up for years, and there was a lot to go through. Decisions had to be made regarding each item. I'd be holding a bill for uncle Gerald's dry cleaning, dated 1945, from a firm in Delhi: did I keep it or not? Here's a mathematics exercise book of Flo's from when she was ten, does it stay or does it go into the recycling? Every decision was painstakingly slow because of a laborious totting-up procedure involved in the decision-making process. This invariably came down to one metric: how much emotional value will this item have in 50 years' time, compared to the weight involved in keeping it?

After working on the house in the morning, I spent the second half of the day working on the Mac, producing stories for the property firm. It was good to concentrate on other topics for a while but in the evenings it all came home to me: whether I'd be able to hold on to the house, whether I'd make it in the property sector, whether the kids were okay, and what sort of man I was to be in such a troubling situation. Hadn't my parents scrimped and saved to send me to boarding school, where I'd received an education fit for a captain of industry? Wasn't I from good family, so why was I now was letting everyone down? Perhaps I was an arrogant little shit, as Tilly had semi-jokingly – but frequently – called me at the *News*. Wasn't I so up myself that I had turned down a perfectly reasonable job offer from my editor with a "tut" – what sort of entitled prick does that?

During this time friends and family were amazing. You really find out a lot more about people once you're not cushioned from the outside world by a large organisation. And about yourself: you appreciate things like good, nourishing food, honest conversation, far more. And if your wellbeing isn't coming from within for the moment, you still have choices. It doesn't help if you gorge out on pizza and beer every day. Things like caffeine intake, sugar intake, exercise, positive interactions, healthy relationships… you still exercise choice about the minutiae of your feelings, your decisions make the difference between success and failure, and even if you know you're a busted flush in one department that doesn't mean you shut down and give up on others. On the contrary, that's when you have to dig deep, and work out new ways to tap your own resourcefulness.

There were also a whole lot of responsibilities that had been sidelined over the years, so this was a good time to spend time with people long cared about and trusted. All the signs were that it was time for a whole new level of ugly on the world stage. The nightmare of Brexit was starting to make itself felt, earlier in the year Donald Trump had moved into the White House, and China and Russia were resurgent. But when I made an inventory of my life the brood was top of the list.

Flo by now was living in Vlaardingen with Thijs: I was really happy how well everything was going for her in the Netherlands, Thijs' family being absolutely delightful and her role as communications officer at the Network of Wellbeing (based in Totnes, Devon) allowing her to contribute to an increasingly vibrant sector. Charlie had been to India twice since leaving college: incredibly, he'd visited Dharamshala and met my friend and teacher Baba's wife Kailash, aged 90, which opened a door that can never be closed. He was now set up in Madrid and loving Spanish culture, and regularly performing at bars and clubs with his guitar outside of his day job teaching English. Emily, however, was a concern because she was living in a co-operative community in Mill Road and I'd effectively lost touch with her. Ironic, to be in day-to-day contact via Skype and WhatsApp with Flo and Chas overseas, yet to have lost contact with a daughter who lived in the same town. Ironic, and saddening. Repairing the relationship was a first priority, and it wasn't going to be easy. An estrangement had taken place nine months before, when Emily had moved out of the family home. Since then, there had been very little contact, except briefly over Christmas.

The first step involved a regular meet-up every week for lunch or afternoon tea, and after a few weeks there were visits to help sort things out in the house. Emily had published one book and had written a second: she worked hard promoting them. However her living arrangements were a bit chaotic and it seemed to be a good idea for her to have the opportunity of staying at the family home as and when required. Gradually, there was progress.

At some point that summer I attended an appointment at one of the NHS' cognitive behaviour units. I sat in the waiting room, and the room gradually filled up with a surprising demographic of people. None was over 40. Two were probably in their 20s, and two 35-40ish, the rest were early-30s young women. Professional women, such as one would see any day of the week on any of the science parks dotted around the city. And there was me thinking they were in great jobs, having a great time all the time. And maybe they do have great jobs but the cost, the hidden cost to individual wellbeing, of life at this incredibly intense point in global history is very high. Nothing is ever going to be good enough, and it could all be swept aside in a nuclear winter or a few more years of climate breakdown. First-world problems? The problems are real, but young people have never been told that always being selfie-ready, with a great job, in a fantastic relationship and having expensive fun 24/7 carries an unaffordable price tag.

A generation of young people are not just being allowed, but are being *encouraged*, to incubate serious wellbeing and mental health issues as a result of the speed of change in the 21st century and not enough is being done to address the problem. The next generation is expected to deal with climate disaster, a post-oil energy crisis, mass species extinction, a food crisis, a possible antibiotics crisis, a probable water crisis and ecological breakdown with an economy entirely unsuited to resolving the challenges.

Life is a multi-faceted affair and time brings all sorts of changes, 'twas ever thus and we'd be naive if we didn't think other generations never faced civilisation-ending prospects. In fact, it's been pretty much civilisation-ending prospects from day one, when we were competing for advantage with neanderthals and the denisovans and had to work out how to act as a group to survive. We're still on that road, trying to work as a group to survive, but the skills that made us better hunters and then better farmers aren't the skills this generation needs. The fact is that we've not made any provision for future challenges. Society has failed a whole generation, saddling them with impossible expectations, then sniping at them on the way down for failing to uphold the aspirational achievements they've being browbeaten to aim for.

Looking around, I saw so many people facing far worse and not getting any support. It felt like a hidden epidemic had been unleashed on the population and I started to fret more about outcomes for everyone I knew. By this time that included Jo's fourth child, the kids' half-sister, Aggie, who was now in more regular contact.

Aggie had been adopted when she was five. The adoption agency allowed a letter or card to be exchanged once a year until she was 18, at which point she had the opportunity to meet her half-sisters and half-brother. It turned out she had been living a few miles away all the time. In the end the meet-up occurred spontaneously: they had a mutual friend who went to college with Charlie and worked with Aggie on the punt service which operated along the river Cam. They were introduced at the Cambridge Beer Festival in 2011, to much amazement and delight.

I met Aggie and her adoptive father a few months later at a launch for Emily's first book, "The Religion of Self-Enlightenment". The existing system is broken, was Emily's take on the world she found herself in. Her determination to seek a better path has to be respected. From the poets and the maverick philosophers come the stories that we need: where are their voices? They have been marginalised in the headlong rush for a future we haven't tried to visualise or shape, that is being devised for us by self-interested others, and yet we all know that the future will be defined by nature's response to the continued indignities piled upon it.

Bit by bit, with a new (plant-based) diet, meditation, exercise and reduced screen time, the bad nights receded and a more restorative nocturnal pattern resumed, though it still seems to me that a good night's sleep is a gift, not a right.

– Chapter 33 –

Summer came, the house was nowhere near ready for me to go to Madagascar, and I was fighting for my professional life. Although I was writing on an unpaid freelance basis for various publications, it began to feel like I was losing the battle in the property sector. The property market was not a good fit for me. This was brought home in two situations.

In the first I interviewed an alms house clerk who was making some of the alms houses on his patch available to younger people. Alms houses are traditionally for the elderly but the idea here was that a younger section of society would pay very little rent and therefore could save up to get on to the property ladder.

The story didn't appear on the property website I was paid to populate. I didn't upload the stories myself, I sent them to the firm's HQ in London. There was no explanation as to why the almshouse story was unsuitable, but I knew why: property developers don't like cheap rents, they like to extract the maximum market value from the properties they build, so they get the profits they want. Whether they acknowledge it or not, they expect the tab for the social impact of their behaviour to be picked up by the state. Almshouses were associated with the very poor, and it was tricky to think that prices were now so high that buying a home was unaffordable for families with young children. Stories about the downside of the property bubble in Cambridge were not welcome.

Then, in the summer, came the Grenfell Tower disaster, when 71 people died in a blaze at a London tower block. The tragedy spelled out that there were two types of people in the

UK: property owners and non-property owners. Property developers, and the market which serves them – of which I was a part – don't want to be reminded of the way the customers of their customers get treated. That's not how they wish to portray their brand.

When I realised that my ability to write freely was a (self-created) illusion, and that what I was doing was closer to a PR/marketing role rather than a journalistic one, I started scaling back my involvement. It was more visceral than that though, it got to the point where I physically couldn't write: I had nothing to say to the property sector. I would sit at the computer and invent a ton of excuses and distractions to avoid doing what I was supposed to do, until one month I said I wasn't going to submit an invoice because I hadn't done any work and that was that. I've nothing against ownership of property as such but the division between property have's and have-not's is souring society. Today the average Londoners spends 60 per cent of his or her wages on rent, and something is very wrong about that. In the last 30 years Cambridge has become a property Mecca, but the fact that the city has the biggest ratio of homeless people in the UK is a by-the-by to developers: from their point of view, this was no time to be developing a social conscience.

To survive in an ever more complex economic environment, people are compartmentalising their thinking. When this compartmentalisation process goes too far it results in a lack of compassion. Without compassion, who or what are we?

I was running out of road. I was applying for other jobs but they mostly involved only some aspects of my skill set, usually in a marketing or communications context, and although anything would have been preferable to working in the property sector, I wasn't getting offers. But of course, this was a town that had two local newspapers. So what about the *Cambridge Independent* – might that not be a good fit?

It was time to reconcile my own thoughts and feelings on the city's newest paper. Hadn't I just left a company I'd worked for 20 years, and here I was, a couple of months later, thinking to knock on the door of a rival and ask for a job? Where was my loyalty to the company which had kept me going from the time I'd rocked up, 20 years previously, a disaster area, close to unemployable: hadn't they done right, give or take, by me for two decades?

However, I needed to think clearly. Maybe it was wrong to think of the *Cambridge Independent* as a rival – maybe it was just an alternative. *Cambridge News* was now absolutely geared towards the website, and the *Cambridge Independent* had made it clear that it believed print still had a future, which was a very positive development in an industry shorn of optimism and investment. Could it be that the digital tide would turn, and people would continue to buy newspapers? Could I possibly contribute to it in some way?

I talked it over with colleagues and former colleagues: Jenny, William, Adam, Maria, my sisters and others, who all pointed out that any loyalty I owed the *News* was cancelled out by the way the new owners had treated me. No one will think badly of you, Jenny assured me, you wouldn't be betraying your old comrades by going to work across the road, they'll be glad for you. I hoped she was right. Loyalty is a big deal for me, but I was a free agent, and showing loyalty to people who haven't shown you much is unjustifiable sycophancy.

I went to Somerset a couple of times with Emily and spent time with my longtime chum Jaine. Interestingly, her son was living in the same way as Emily: outside the system as much as possible. It was incredible to be in Glastonbury again and consider how each new generation faces new battles. I'd left a doubter 20 years earlier but a lot of faith was restored: each generation finds new nourishment in Avalon, and millennials are very radical thinkers. Where a previous generation had wanted to change the system from within by promoting natural justice and sustainable technology, they want to dump the system altogether and start over. I still like to think the worst excesses of climate change can be averted, but it's gone from a reasonable assumption to a long shot in a matter of two decades.

Just after I got back from a visit to Somerset I spotted an event going on at Cambridge United Football Club, which is a mile or so away from home. It was a *Cambridge Independent* networking event, and I decided I'd go along in my property role and say hello to the folks there. Who knows who I'd bump into?

The occasion was a lot of fun and it was really good to be able to meet up with people I knew and liked. It was liberating not to have to represent *Cambridge News* and to realise I liked people because they were good people, not because they worked for this organisation or that organisation. Keeping an open mind about the *Cambridge Independent* was a good idea. I hadn't seen Paul Brackley there, but I'd asked about him. I thought maybe I'd drop him an email and congratulate him on the paper winning two weekly newspaper awards in its first year. It was a pretty impressive start.

So that's what I did and a couple of weeks later I got a call from Paul saying he was sorry to have missed me at the networking event and would I like to drop by for a chat? So one Friday I popped over to the Iliffe offices in Milton. There were some generalities about how the paper was doing, and some suggestion that there would be some freelance work at some point in the near future, but nothing specific until the conversation was pretty much wrapped up and then Paul said: "By the way, what are you doing on Monday?"

Monday was a bank holiday and I was due to have a late lunch with my dear friend from Cape Town, Liane, who is Adam's mum. It was also a bank holiday, which no one wants to work on. And it was in the middle of a glorious summer.

"Sure, I'm available Monday, Paul," I said.

"Oh good, well if you could come in and do some production work that would be very welcome," he said.

"Excellent, what time would you like me to start?"

The details were arranged and Paul spent half an hour talking me through the system as I made notes. I walked out feeling pretty good about the way it went. I knew Paul well enough to realise that the important bit, for him, was could I work at short notice, that Monday. Did I want to work or did I want to deal in generalities? I wanted to work.

The Monday shift went well, after a slow start trying to get to grips with the computer system. Fortunately it was Atex-based, and only a bit customised. By midday it was like I'd climbed back on a bicycle and was off down the lanes. More shifts followed, and then some writing work started coming my way too. Everyone at the *Cambridge Independent* worked unbelievably hard, especially Paul, who was writing prolifically as well as getting involved in all the other responsibilities facing the editor of a new title. It was fantastic to be working for a news organisation that was expanding rather than savagely contracting.

It turned out to be a good summer. Charlie came over from Madrid for three months, and it was great to hang out and play table tennis with him. He was due to work and stay at an international school in town. When he got to town he said he was worried about not speaking Spanish for the months he was away from Spain, and joined a community that met up to practice speaking Spanish. That was how he met Maite, and Maite became his partner: she being from a Basque family in northern Spain and working at Addenbrooke's Hospital in Cambridge. The irony of a lad from Cambridge working in Spain meeting a Spanish girl working in Cambridge, the very modernity of it! Flo came over twice, once for a week as a stopover to an event in Totnes, and once to spend time with her sister.

To cap it all, one evening I got a call from Russ at the *News*. There were some shifts going on the production hub, he said. Would I like to give it a go? It turned out that the new editor of the print section, Julie, was off on long-term sick leave and that meant Russ was in charge.

I'd been proud to have been a chum of Russ' over many years and it was an honour to accept his invitation, though when I went back to the *News* I was shocked at the changes in just three months. When you leave a home or a job or a marriage where you've created many memories, you think of the people you knew as still being there somehow, of how things were when they were fun, but so many more people had left it was impossible to sustain that illusion. And still they were still closing departments down. Alice Ryan, the supremely elegant features editor, I'd last seen on my leaving day, when she was teary about my departure because we'd become chums only relatively recently: the next time I saw her it was her leaving day. Fortunately though, she later went to work at the *Cambridge Independent*, where she now edits the award-winning *Velvet* magazine.

The *News'* features desk kept only one person, Emily Martin – everyone else was made redundant or made offers that they had to refuse. It was good that Emily survived, but it didn't make up for the loss of Alice Ryan or my old commercial features mucker Lisa Millard or Lydia Fallon or Jude Clarke or Louise Moore or Emma Higginbotham or Ella Walker – nothing and no one could make up for them.

The design department was another hub shut down at the *News*, which meant another bleak day saying goodbye to Vanessa Holmes, who had been at the firm for 20 years, and Debbie Rodman. Even the great Andrew Ormiston was cast into the wilderness, though it was a delight to see him in the *Cambridge Independent* newsroom for some shifts later in the autumn. The sports desk, showing something of the Druid collectivism that Jenny had suggested bound them together, all left too, some for other jobs and some just to try something or anything somewhere else. And at the end of summer John Meredith, the sub who was already a legend when I'd arrived

21 years before, also handed his notice in. I was doing a freelance shift the day he announced his departure: there was a lot of respect for him that he hadn't waited to get a redundancy cheque, he left on his own terms: it was yet another "end of an era" situation.

Overall it was good to go back, though. It helped settle some ghosts. It was like revisiting another world, and a life you remembered with fondness, a life you missed, with smart people and some cool skills. And some genuine characters. But when I got back, they weren't there any more, apart from Jenny, the always-wonderful chief reporter Chris Elliott and Raymond the crime reporter, along with relative newcomers like Matthew. There was no nourishment there, no spark, not at that time. It had moved on, the circus, the sideshows, the great teeming masses of people who'd populated the great ship *Cambridge News*, all departed for shores near and far, certain and uncertain. The newsroom was terribly, eerily, quiet, and those left behind were shell-shocked, and understandably so. The advertising folk were thinner on the ground too: just Tilly, who had moved on to the events team, and a handful of others. Her chum Emily had long since left, first to work in Dubai, before returning to the UK to work for the *Cambridge Independent.*

It's people who make a company a great place to work: take them away and you've just got a collection of ageing computers and some strip lighting in an out-of-town office block. By the end of summer the freelance shifts ended. The freelance budget was zeroed out, and I left the *News* for the second and final time. It didn't hurt nearly so much though.

Later in the year, Jenny retired. *Cambridge Business* magazine was closed – the last edition was in August 2017 – which meant her entire workload would be directed towards producing digital clickbait. A few weeks after she heard of the closure she went off sick with a trapped nerve in her back, and one day she made an appointment to see the editor and told him that she wanted to retire "with immediate effect". Jenny had been through the whole works in the last few years: she'd left her husband after discovering he was having an affair he was unwilling to break off, moved from Royston to Cambridge, to a great little house near the river Cam, and had a new partner, Richard, a semi-retired GP. Earlier in the year her divorce settlement had come through so she was financially stable, and she was due to marry Richard at the end of the year. She was preparing to retire the following year in any case.

It was great she left on her own terms too.

– Postscript –

As I write the news is all over town: journalists are an endangered species. Partly that's because of the internet, but it's also because journalists haven't been fighting back, not putting their case to the court of public opinion, and the irony of the under-reporting of journalism's agonies has been what this book has been all about.

The industry's woes, to whatever extent self-inflicted, are considerable but at least we now know that without accountability and transparency for those in positions of power, the world is a much more dangerous place.

The Grenfell Tower tragedy in London happened because the cladding used on the tower block was illegal in many countries and inflammable in all of them. This was known before the fire, but when residents tried to publicise their concerns about the cladding that was to kill so many of them, no one looked into their claims. Part of that was because the local press didn't take up take their story. It wasn't so much a case of being asleep at the wheel, as having been mugged, dragged out of the car and thrown into a ditch. It's probably true to say that bankers have been saturated with public anger in recent years, while property developers have inexplicably been let off rather easy.

The current vogue for turning newsrooms into word farms will come to an end some day. In the meantime the winners are the politicians and business leaders who can look after number one without being obliged to answer for their excesses, and the losers are everyone else. The outcome is that the unfairness and injustices of the skewed capitalism practiced in the early 21st century remain largely unchallenged.

The situation was described rather well by *Brighton Argus* editor Mike Gilson who wrote an editorial headlined 'Why journalists must always be a nuisance' in which he said: "It is not healthy for any journalist to have too cosy a relationship with the leaders in our community, its institutions, the movers and shakers if you like.

"Respectful yes. Give credit of course. But simply become a vehicle for unchallenged views as some media outlets seem to be today? No.

"Readers can get the press releases online from source anyway so what need of the middle man, ie the media?

"Journalists are outsiders. The safeguards that govern democracy demands it be thus. Show me an editor who wines and dines regularly with the powerful, or with whom they are on constant speed dial and I'll show you someone who doesn't really understand the job.

"Journalists, post-Leveson inquiry, are not exactly clutched to the nation's bosom at present. But their role in society is worthy of debate.

"Forgive me for sounding pompous about my own trade, but if journalism is to survive the communications revolution we are all living through it must be clear-eyed about its purpose.

"If it is not it will have no right to thrive and at local level, where we all live after all, the democratic deficit will be real."

People are starting to realise that newspapers have been bent to the will of their owners, and to the will of corporate interests. In allowing this to take place, Parliament has let democracy down.

Audiences are wising up to the difference between the truth and fake news/'alternative facts' which is good news but, for newspapers, the riddle remains: the key to future prospects is establish a way to make money from digital content. Finding a industry-wide payment method acceptable to all parties remains elusive. Whether – and how much, and how – readers are prepared to pay for news is a challenge that should exercise the minds of all who would see the democratic process survive.

Even if news will always be available somewhere online for free, the analysis and interpretation of news is subject to the same clunky models as news, even though these more studied reports could – and, arguably, should – be better monetised. Not every news provider offers commentary on the news, and not every commentator is able to develop a readership base, but there is a market for quality and there is considerable, yet unevaluated, scope for a billing system that bypasses the need for subscription paywalls. Commentator journalists such as George Monbiot, Robert Fisk, Jeremy Clarkson, Peter Hitchens, Max Hastings, Suzanne Moore, Richard Littlejohn, John Pilger, Yanis Varoufakis and Andrew Rawnsley all have distinctive voices, voices which are monitored closely by their readers. Yet there they are, dished up for nothing on a one-size-fits-all free platform.

When you look at the way the music industry has adapted to the internet, you can see the pivot: last century the bulk of musicians' and performers' wealth came via CD sales, and concerts were a loss leader. Now, the revenue stream from

CDs has been replaced by trickles from downloads and streaming, and the live arena is where the money is. The newspaper industry needs its own pivot.

For more than a decade it was hoped the impasse at the frontier of paid-for journalism would be resolved, but now it is later, and the next stop is "too late". Facebook has changed the algorithms for publishers who post their on its platform, further damaging an already modest revenue stream. This trend, to marginalise external news sources or oblige content organisations to pay to post content, will continue. The fightback has no time to lose and hopefully, in the wake of the Cambridge Analytica revelations, people now understand what's at stake.

As Noah Yuval Harari, the author of "A Brief History of Mankind", said in an interview for *Handelsblatt Global* in late 2017: "We are now experiencing the confluence of two immense scientific revolutions: the first in biology and the second in computer science. And when you put the two together, when biotech and infotech merge, what you get is the ability to design life, to control life."

I'm very lucky to work in a city where biotech and infotech are being progressed every day, and I have to point out that there are some scary implications and choices being made. Some of the biggest questions in AI and genetics are being road-mapped in this otherwise-quiet part of East Anglia. Society needs a proper conversation about genetic and AI. What's happening in Cambridge deserves proper press coverage – and scrutiny. I've been lucky – and am grateful – to have been allowed to develop roles at the *Cambridge News* and subsequently at the *Cambridge*

Independent, whose remit is to cover the astonishing developments happening under our noses in this university city and tech/pharma hub every day of the week, probably every hour if you drill down enough. And being able to cover them in some depth is an absolute delight.

The wider danger is that smoke and mirrors of politics and economic activity has obscured fundamental questions. Perhaps that's the purpose of smokescreens, but openly debating the issues we face as a species is now fundamental to our survival. As the whirlwinds of artificial intelligence and genomics advance, the media needs to be fully engaged in what is happening at all stages of the journey. This includes writing about what could, might and even should happen next. To deliver this mission, journalism needs to be properly funded: the day that journalists receive full and proper payment for posting their content on the world wide web can't come soon enough.

At the same time, journalism must be confronted with some awkward questions. To what extent did the media facilitate fake news and 'alternative facts'? Why were there no whistleblowers during the phone hacking scandal? Why has the press in this country failed to offer a detailed fact-checking service on the lies and distortions of Brexit or Trumpism? What is the role of the press in propping up corporate interests?

The powerful have always been driven to manipulate events, and where events and agendas are obscured in a media-obsessed, internet-driven, age, tough questions must be asked. And the worry is that there's not enough people around to push back on the reverses suffered by the fourth estate in the new, digitally-driven, century.

Every journalistic generation has to learn to be fearless, to show bravery under fire whether literal or intellectual, to ask pertinent questions and to retain balance so that they're responding to readers' interests and right to know, not just to the whims of the market. It's not easy, and the process needs assistance from the public: not charity, but support. Journalism is like food: if you eat junk food you get zero nutrition and you run the risk of ingesting lots of ingredients that can do you harm.

The challenges are significant, but not insuperable. The first port of call is that you, the reader, identify when you're being lied to and treated like a fool, and stop buying into it. The #StopFundingHate campaign has shown how this can work. The second port of call is that all internet publishers be obliged to create a business platform that's on a level playing field – that they all do what newspapers do, and check each page for accuracy before it's published.

Checking content before it is published is anathema to executives at Facebook or Google, but right now the costs of the hatred, lies and propaganda they allow to appear on their sites are entirely borne by the taxpayer. It is the taxpayer who pays for the police and legal services to sort out whether or not content contravenes the law: this cost should be borne by internet publishers, just as it is by newspaper publishers, who invest in a complex and expensive system of checks before publication. The answer is not for publishers to cut out the fact-checkers, but to oblige all content publishers to check content before it is posted. There should be no exceptions when it comes to paying your way in business, and allowing Silicon Valley firms to get away with a low-tax zero-responsibility model for their antics has proved disastrous for society as an entity. This business model is predicated on taking no responsibility nor paying any tax for the content on their platforms. That must change.

If Google and Facebook continue to have their way there will be no money for education, or health, or the police, or anything else the government does. That's wrong, and the next generation will suffer agonies as the scale of the divestment in their futures becomes apparent. Exporting wealth to tax havens is ruining nation states. The wiring for the new era has been highjacked by Silicon Valley, and the level of accountability is dangerously low.

Even a cursory look at the history of humans shows that this is a species capable of acting together when facing the most extreme threats.

Consider 'The Blue Planet Effect', the result of a David Attenborough documentary series which brought the issue of plastic in the food chain to the attention of the public. Within months, solutions to curb plastic consumption began to be put in place. In terms of the drama of climate change, and the challenges in agriculture, technology, democracy, medicine, education and finance, the media's role is to truthfully report the facts. Journalism has the power to explain, outline, educate, inform, celebrate, cherish, amuse and illuminate the world we're in. It's had a shaky start to the digital age, but all is not lost. It just needs to be properly funded, and that's as much to do with inspiring readers to buy newspapers as it is to do with the industry finding a unified voice.

In the meantime a lot of good people have left the trade. Many former colleagues left to develop careers elsewhere; some left for other titles, be they newspapers or magazines. Some retired, and some just took a break from it all. Some are still waiting for the phone to ring, but whatever, I have huge respect and admiration for all my former colleagues and wish them every success with whatever they're doing now.

In April 2018 *Cambridge News'* chief reporter, Chris Elliott, took voluntary redundancy. He had started his career at the paper 32 years previously, when newspapers were entirely embedded in the analogue era. With his departure the last surviving link to the pre-digital era was severed.

In the same month the *Cambridge Independent,* described by judges as "a magnificent stitched and trimmed magazine-style weekly", retained its 'UK Weekly Newspaper of the Year' title at the national NewsAwards 2018.

Printed in Poland
by Amazon Fulfillment
Poland Sp. z o.o., Wrocław